cool Irish names

FOR BABIES

ST. MARTIN'S GRIFFIN
NEW YORK

cool Irish names

FOR BABIES

PAMELA REDMOND SATRAN
& LINDA ROSENKRANTZ

COOL IRISH NAMES FOR BABIES. Copyright © 2009 by Pamela Redmond Satran and Linda Rosenkrantz. All rights reserved. Printed in the United States of America. For information, address St. Martin's Press, 175 Fifth Avenue, New York, N.Y. 10010.

www.stmartins.com

Library of Congress Cataloging-in-Publication Data

Satran, Pamela Redmond.
   Cool Irish names for babies / Pamela Redmond Satran and Linda Rosenkrantz.—1st ed.
      p. cm.
  Includes index.
  ISBN-13: 978-0-312-53912-2
  ISBN-10: 0-312-53912-6
  1. Names, Personal—United States. 2. Names, Personal—Ireland. 3. Names, Irish. I. Rosenkrantz, Linda. II. Title.
  CS2377.S2652 2009
  929.4'4—dc22

2008037583

Portions of this book appeared in an earlier form in *Beyond Shannon & Sean: An Enlightened Guide to Irish Baby Naming*. Copyright © 1992 by Linda Rosenkrantz and Pamela Redmond Satran.

First Edition: March 2009

10 9 8 7 6 5 4 3 2 1

contents

pre-cool cool
OLD NAMES

new cool
CREATIVE NAMES

introduction

What does cool mean when it comes to Irish names for babies?

Something very different from what it means for other kinds of baby names.

Our original American *Cool Names for Babies* includes thousands of names that are invented, drawn from a range of ethnic backgrounds, borrowed from places or surnames or things. When it comes to cool names in general, anything from Heaven to Harlow to Harmony goes.

The British are more conservative, so when we devised the UK edition of *Cool Names,* we focused on the revival of such old-fashioned names as Edith and Arthur, on trendy short forms such as Dixie and Alfie, on royal names like Leonie and Ludovic.

And then we came to the Irish. Irish baby-naming is a culture unto itself, full of gorgeous and often obscure ancient names whose original bearers were kings and queens, mythological heroes and heroines, saints and fairies. Irish parents today have fully embraced traditional names, elevating such native choices as Aoife and Niamh, Cian and Caoimhe and Cillian, Oisín and Róisín, Darragh and

Aisling and Saoirse to the top of the popularity charts with non-Irish names popular throughout the English-speaking world: Emma, Sophie, and Ava for girls; Jack, Daniel, and Luke for boys.

Irish-American baby names are a somewhat different story. Names of immigrant ancestors—Bridget and Nora, Patrick and Mickey—morphed over the years to such '50s faux-Irish favorites as Colleen and Doreen and Noreen. The most recent wave of Irish names popular in the United States are surname-names for girls and boys alike: Delaney and Conor, Riley and Rowan.

Which brings us back to the issue of cool.

Cool, when we're talking about Irish names, most often means traditional. In many ways, what's old in Irish names *is* what's new. The coolest names these days are the most deeply rooted ones: Finn, for instance, the name of the greatest hero of Irish mythology, Finn McCool. Or Rory, perhaps spelled the Irish way, Ruairi.

If distinctive undiscovered names often count for cool, you'll find them all in these pages, along with details about why their original bearers were so inspirational. Irish literature and theater also offer a trove of stylish names with inspiring associations, along with lots of other sources, both expected and surprising. And if, in the past, you've been somewhat put off by the challenges of confusing Irish pronunciations, have no fear: we've provided specific phonetic spellings next to every possibly problematic name.

The following are some basic rules to keep in mind when searching for a cool Irish name for your baby.

COOL MEANS UNUSUAL

In general, the more unusual a name, the cooler it is. With once-uncommon Irish names such as Liam, Conor, and Riley now competing for the top spots, you have to move further and further from the mainstream to find a name that's truly distinctive. While fashionable names such as Delaney and Reagan may still be wonderful choices (and perhaps ultimately the right ones for you), you can't really call them cool. The coolest Irish names now are those that push the envelope in all sorts of ways: Maguire and O'Brien, for instance, and Grainne and Senan.

COOL IS DIVERSE

Using a distinctly Irish name is a cool thing to do in this age of celebrating diversity and being proud of your ethnic heritage. Still, Irish names don't have a monopoly on cool, and you may wish to search farther afield for fresh choices. But you don't have to go too far: Names from other Celtic cultures—Scottish and Welsh and Cornish and Breton—might provide the individuality you crave without sacrificing too much tradition. And if your tastes run more toward the pan-cultural Emma and Edward end of the spectrum, we've included those here, too.

COOL GOES BEYOND CONVENTION

You may want to explore some fresh sources for Irish names with cultural resonance. Hero names—borne by politicians and poets—you might not have considered as first names are one idea. Irish last names are another, and not just the usual suspects such as

Kelly and Ryan but Tierney and Magee and Sullivan as well. Irish place names can be yet another new locale in which to search for first names. And Irish words can be turned into names, too.

COOL DRAWS ON POPULAR CULTURE

The world is full of inspiration for cool baby-naming—and more full every day, thanks to the innovative names of characters in films and books and to the names of starbabies and celebrities themselves. In these pages you'll find a rundown of the coolest Irish names in modern literature and film, and of the stars and their children who influence baby-naming style.

DON'T BE AFRAID OF COOL

When today's parents were growing up, if you had an unusual name, other kids thought you were a bit odd. But now that the concept of cool permeates the culture, with so many people from celebrities to the other kids in the classroom bearing unusual names, children are more apt to admire distinctive names than to ridicule them.

THERE'S MORE THAN ONE WAY TO BE COOL

Cool wouldn't be cool if it was too regimented. There are cool names to suit any sensibility or level of cool, from the mainstream to the avant-garde. How far you want to go depends on your taste, your sense of adventure, your community. Before you settle at either end of the spectrum or on one particular name, weigh the various options and become comfortable with the brand and level of cool that fit you best.

COOL ISN'T EVERYTHING

So what if you're one of those people who realize that a cool name isn't for you or your child? What if you read this book and find yourself intrigued, entertained, inspired . . . but in the end a lot more convinced than you realized that you want to give your child a plain, solid, and decidedly uncool name such as Shannon or Sean?

So what, indeed. A name is not your personal style statement, a choice with which to impress the world. Rather, you should think of it as something that will identify your child for the rest of his or life, a label he or she will have to live with forever. You may decide that cool is a desirable component of such a lifelong imprimatur. But then again, you may decide that, when it comes to a name, you want nothing to do with cool. (Just know you may have to suffer the consequences when your child is a teenager.)

Whether or not you end up with a cool name, you owe it to your baby and your choice of a name to read this book. For one thing, you'll find hundreds and hundreds of naming options here that you won't find anywhere else, and that will open your eyes to a way of thinking about names that no other book or source can offer. And you'll know for certain, after reading this book, what constitutes a cool name—even if you decide that uncool is cool enough for you.

pop cool

MAINSTREAM NAMES

riley

For many years, lively Irish names have been a prime export to the UK and the U.S.—dating back to the eras of Bridget, Kathleen and Eileen, Kevin, Kelly, Brian, Shannon, and Sean. The last couple of decades have seen a new, ever-increasing burst of popularity of Irish names as reflected in the latest report from the Social Security Administration of the top names in the United States. Below are the names with Irish brogues currently on those lists, starting with the most popular and including old persistent favorites like Ryan and Brian, newer and cooler entries like Maeve and Kellen, hip surnames like Finnegan and Sullivan, and those that have become unisex, such as Riley and Finley.

THE TOP IRISH NAMES IN THE USA

girls

RILEY	ERIN
KENNEDY	REAGAN/REGAN
KEIRA/KIERA	DELANEY

CASSIDY	BRIAN/BRYAN
KELLY	LIAM
McKENNA	BRADY
CAITLIN	BRODY
CIARA	RILEY/REILLY
BRIDGET	PATRICK
TEAGAN	COLIN
KATHLEEN	NOLAN
SHANNON	SHAWN
RYAN	SHANE
CASEY	DONOVAN
AILEEN	BRENDAN
TARA	KEEGAN/KEAGAN
QUINN	QUINN
MAEVE	BRENNAN
KEELY	CASEY
FINLEY	GRADY
IRELAND	DECLAN
SHEA	DARREN
	ROWAN

boys

AIDAN/AIDEN	FINN
RYAN	SHAUN
BRANDON	MICHEAL (Irish spelling)
KEVIN	KELLEN
CONNOR/CONNER/CONOR	MILO
SEAN	RONAN
	BLAINE

KIERAN	SEAMUS
TYRONE	CULLEN
FINNEGAN	FINLEY
KEENAN	RORY
BECKETT	KILLIAN
SULLIVAN	REAGAN

baltimore bridgets & seattle seans

IRISH-AMERICAN POPULAR NAMES

More than four million Irish people immigrated to the United States between 1820 to 1920, contributing their names to the American lexicon. In that century before the uprising of Irish nationalism, most of those names were English ones: Mary and James, Anne and John. Those immigrants who did have typically Irish names—the Bridgets and the Patricks—often sought to trade them in for something less green, with Bridget becoming Bertha or Bernice, Patrick calling himself Pete.

It was with pet forms that the new Irish-Americans first established their distinct naming identity. These were linked closely with the old sod by the 1920s, many of which sound fresh and even cool again today, including the following:

ANNIE	FANNY
BARNEY	FRANNY
BEA	JACK
BERNIE	JENNY
BRIDIE	JOSIE

KATE	MOLLY
KATIE	NED
KAY	NELL/NELLIE
KITTY	NORA
LIZZIE	PADDY
MAC	PAT
MAGGIE	PATSY
MAMIE	PEGGY
MAY	ROSIE
MICKEY	SALLY
MIKE	TESS
MINNIE	TILLIE

Kathleen was one of the first Irish names to come to America, in the nineteenth century, but it wasn't until the 1940s and '50s that the *een* names became truly popular. These included:

AILEEN	KATHLEEN
AIDEEN	MAUREEN
COLLEEN	NOREEN
EILEEN	PEGEEN
DOREEN	ROSALEEN
JOSEPHINE	

Other names with Irish roots popular in mid-twentieth-century America included:

BARRY	MONICA
BERNADETTE	MURIEL
BRIAN	MYRNA
DARRIN/DARREN	NEIL
DEIRDRE	PATRICIA
DENNIS	SHEILA
DUANE	TERRY
KEELEY	TRACY
KEVIN	TYRONE
MONA	

The sexually liberated 1960s and '70s were the perfect time for a certain kind of energetic but informal Irish name. Among those that first found favor in that era, some of which are still used for babies, are:

BRENDAN	RORY
CASEY	RYAN
COREY	SEAN
ERIN	SHANE
KELLY	SHANNON
KERRY	SHAWN
MEGAN	STACY

conor

TOPS IN IRELAND

For many people, Irish and others alike, there's nothing cooler than a popular name, subscribing to the theory that a popular name makes a child feel popular—accepted and approved—having a name that's familiar to all and currently in style. Here then, from the Central Statistics Office in Dublin, are the current Top 50 names in Ireland, including some that have hardly been heard here, which increases their cool factor considerably:

boys	girls
JACK	SARAH
SEAN	EMMA
CONOR	ELLA
DANIEL	KATIE
JAMES	SOPHIE
ADAM	AVA
RYAN	AOIFE (EE-fa)
LUKE	EMILY

CIAN (KEE-an)	GRACE
MICHAEL	KATE
DYLAN	AMY
AARON	CIARA (KEER-a)
DARRAGH (DA-ra)	HANNAH
THOMAS	LUCY
MATTHEW	CHLOE
DAVID	LEAH
JAMIE	CAOIMHE (KEE-va)
OISIN (OH-sheen)	NIAMH (Neev)
PATRICK	RACHEL
ALEX	ANNA
JOHN	JESSICA
CILLIAN (KILL-ee-an)	LAUREN
EVAN	MOLLY
EÓIN (OH-in)	MIA
SHANE	REBECCA
LIAM	SAOIRSE (SEER-sha)
BEN	RÓISÍN (Ro-SHEEN)
JAKE	LILY
JOSHUA	ABBIE
MARK	MEGAN
HARRY	ELLIE
FIONN (FIN)	HOLLY
JOSEPH	LAURA
CALLUM	RUBY

SAMUEL	ELLEN
CHARLIE	AISLING (ASH-ling)
NATHAN	ÁINE (AH-nya)
CATHAL (Kah-hal)	NICOLE
KYLE	CLODAGH (KLO-da)
ROBERT	ERIN
CIARÁN (KEER-an)	EVA
RONAN	OLIVIA
ANDREW	ISABELLE
KEVIN	CAITLIN
WILLIAM	ABIGAIL
ETHAN	TARA
TADGH (TYEg)	KATELYN
RORY	AMELIA
NOAH	JULIA
CALUM	SHAUNA

And here are the Top 10 in Northern Ireland, reflecting a somewhat more Anglo-oriented picture:

boys	girls
JACK	KATIE
JAMES	GRACE
MATTHEW	SOPHIE
DANIEL	LUCY
RYAN	EMMA

THOMAS	ELLIE
ADAM	SARAH
JOSHUA	ERIN
DYLAN	HANNAH
BEN	ANNA

ronan

MOVING UP

And which are the names rising fastest up the ladder, those on the cusp of megapopularity in Ireland? In the last year counted, there were several first-timers in the Top 100 list: the six newly arrived girls were Brooke (the greatest rise), Millie, Taylor, Muireann, Freya, and Maya, and the boys' names making their debuts were Rhys, Oliver, Jayden, Louis, Lucas, and Jacob. Other names on the upswing in the Emerald Isle include:

girls

AOIBHINN (EE-veen)

EIMEAR (Ee-mer)

ISABEL

ISOBEL

KATE

LARA

LILY

MAEVE

RUBY

SADHBH (Sive—rhymes with *five*)

SOPHIA

VICTORIA

ZARA

boys

AIDAN

ALAN

CILLIAN (KILL-ee-an)

DIARMAID (DEER-mid)	MAX
EDWARD	ORAN
FINN	OSCAR
GAVIN	RIAN
HARRY	RONAN
KIERAN	TADHG (TYEg)
LIAM	

In Northern Ireland, the fastest-gaining boy's name is Carter, followed by Rory and Aodhan—and for girls, Kayleigh, Lucie, and Poppy are on the rise. And for a local perspective, in the county of Derry, the top names were Callum and Ellie.

keira

In the UK, Irish names, especially for boys, also pop up on the pop lists. Here are the current favorites:

girls	boys
ERIN	RYAN
CAITLIN	LIAM
KEIRA	CONNOR
NIAMH (Neev)	FINLAY/FINLEY
SHANNON	KIERAN
	BRANDON
	RILEY
	AIDAN
	SEAN

darragh

Many Irish names, particularly the surname-names, swing both ways, an increasingly popular method of injecting coolness into your baby's name. While names such as Kerry and Kelly, once used for boys as well as girls, have largely shifted to the female side, a whole new raft of choices has arrived to take their place. Here is a selection of names equally appropriate, not to mention cool, for both girls and boys.

AILBHE (ALL-bay)	**DARRAGH (DA-ra)**
ALBANY	**DELANEY**
BEVIN	**DERRY**
CANICE (Kan-is)	**DONNELLY**
CASEY	**DUFFY**
CASS	**ELATHA (AHL-hah)**
CASSIDY	**EVANY (EV-nee)**
CLANCY	**FALLON**
DARA	**FARRELL**
DARCY	**FINEEN**

FLANAGAN	OWNY
FLANN	QUINN
FLANNERY	REAGAN
FLYNN	RILEY
KENNEDY	RORY
LOGAN	ROWAN
MAGEE	RYAN
MAOLÍOSA (Ma-LEE-sa)	SHEA (Shay)
MORGAN	TIERNAN
MURPHY	TIERNEY

COOLEST
UNISEX NAME
· · ·
Rowan

arwen

PAN-CELTIC COOL

Since Celtic languages have several different branches, you may want to look beyond Irish names to those of your fellow Celts: the Scottish, Welsh, Cornish, Breton, and even the Manx, from the Isle of Man. As with Irish names, many of these are being revived in their native lands, offering the perfect blend of tradition and exotic cool. Note that a few of the boys' names—Dylan, Idris, Reese—would work and perhaps be even cooler for girls.

girls

AALIN (AH-lin)	Manx
AAMOR (AH-mor)	Breton
ADARYN (AH-da-rin)	Welsh
ADO (AY-do)	Cornish
AELA (Ay-la)	Breton
AELWEN (Ay-EL-wen)	Welsh
AERONA (Ay-RO-na)	Welsh
AFTON	Scottish
AILLA (AY-la)	Cornish

AILSA (AYL-sa)	Scottish
AINSLEY (AYNS-lee)	Scottish
ALIENOR (Ai-LIN-or)	Breton
ALMEDA (AL-me-da)	Breton
ANCHORET (AN-kor-et)	Welsh
ANDRAS (AHN-dras)	Cornish
ANEIRA (An-EAR-ra)	Welsh
ANGHARAD (An-GA-rad)	Welsh
ARWEN	Welsh
AZENOR (AH-zen-or)	Breton
BERYAN (BER-yan)	Cornish
BLODWEN (BLOD-wen)	Welsh
BRANWEN (BRAN-wen)	Welsh
BRONWEN	Welsh
BRYONY (BRY-o-nee)	Welsh
CERIDWEN (Ker-id-win)	Welsh
CERYS (Ker-is)	Welsh
CORALIE	Breton
DELWEN (Del-wen)	Welsh
DEMELZA (De-mel-sa)	Cornish
DERRYTH (Derr-ith)	Welsh
DWYN (Dwin)	Welsh
EILWEN (El-win)	Welsh
ELSPETH	Scottish
ELUNED (El-EEN-ed)	Welsh
ENORA (EN-or-a)	Breton
ERTHA	Cornish

ERWANEZ	Breton
FFION (Feen)	Welsh
GAYNOR	Welsh
GETHAN	Welsh
GLENYS, GLYNIS	
(Glen-is, Glin-is)	Welsh
GWANWEN	Welsh
GWEN, WENN	Cornish
GWYNETH	Welsh
HAUDE (Ha-wid)	Breton
IA (Ee-a)	Cornish
INEDA	Cornish
INIRA (In-er-a)	Welsh
IONA, IONE	
(Eye-OH-na, Eye-OH-nee)	Scottish
ISLA (EYE-la)	Scottish
IVORI	Welsh
KATELL	Breton
KERENZA	Cornish
KEW (Kyu)	Cornish
KEYNE (Kane)	Cornish
MABAN	Welsh
MADRUN (MAD-roon)	Cornish
MAILLI (Molly)	Cornish
MEDWENNA (Mid-wen-a)	Welsh
MELLE	Breton
MEREWIN (Mer-i-win)	Cornish

MINIVER	Cornish
MÒRAG (MAW-rack)	Scottish
MWYNEN (Mwin-in)	Welsh
MYFANWY (Muh-VAHN-wee)	Welsh
NERYS (NER-ees)	Welsh
NESTA	Welsh
NEVID(D) (NEV-id)	Cornish, Welsh
NEWLYN	Welsh
NIA	Welsh
NONNA (NAW-nah)	Welsh
OANEZ (WAH-nes)	Breton
OLWEN	Welsh
PIALA (Pee-A-la)	Cornish, Breton
RHEDYN (RAY-deen)	Welsh
RHIAN, RHIANNON	
(REE-an, Ree-a-non)	Welsh
RHIANWEN (Ree-AHN-wen)	Welsh
RHONWEN	Welsh
ROZENN (ROH-zen)	Breton
SCÁTHACH (Ska-ha)	Scottish
SEIRIAN (Sher-ee-an)	Welsh
SERERENA (Sir-er-EE-na)	Cornish
SEVE, SEVA (SAY-va)	Breton
SIÂN (SHAN)	Welsh
TAMSIN (TAM-zin)	Cornish
TANWEN	Welsh
WENN(A)	Cornish

boys

ACCALON (ACK-a-lon)	Breton
ADEON (AH-dion)	Welsh
AED (Ayd)	Welsh
AEL (AH-eel)	Breton
ANGUS	Scottish
ALASDAIR (AL-us-duhr)	Scottish
ALED (A-lid)	Welsh
ALEF	Cornish
ALUN	Welsh
AMATHEON (Ah-MATH-eon)	Welsh
ANEURIN (An-YOUR-in)	Welsh
ANGWYN (ANG-gwin)	Welsh
ANNAN	Scottish
ARDAN	Scottish
ARGYLE	Scottish
ATHOL (Ah-tall)	Scottish
AURON	Welsh
AUSTELL (Os-tell)	Cornish
BAIRD	Scottish
BANADEL	Welsh
BASTIAN (BAS-tee-an)	Breton
BERWIN (Bear-win)	Cornish
BLAZEY (BLAY-zee)	Cornish
BOWEN	Welsh
BRANWELL	Cornish
BRASTIUS (BRAS-tee-us)	Cornish

BRECON (Brek-on)	Welsh
BREIZH (Brez)	Breton
BRICE, BRYCE	Welsh
BRYN (Brin)	Welsh
BUCHANAN	Scottish
CADOC (KAH-doc)	Welsh
CAMBER	Welsh
CANNOCK, KINNOCK	Cornish
CARADOC (KAR-a-dock)	Welsh
CARANTEC (Kar-AN-tek)	Breton
CASWALLAWN (KAS-wal-an)	Welsh
CORENTIN(E) (Kor-en-TAN)	Breton
DAWE (Daw)	Welsh
DENZEL(L)	Cornish
DERRIEN (DAY-ryen)	Breton
DEVI (DAY-vee)	Breton
DOCCO (DOCK-oh)	Cornish
DONAN	Breton
DUGALD (DOO-gald)	Scottish
DRYSTAN	Welsh
DUNCAN	Scottish
DYLAN	Welsh
EDERN (AY-dern)	Cornish
EDRYD (Ed-rid)	Welsh
EIROS (AIR-os)	Welsh
ELFED	Welsh
ELPHIN	Welsh

EMLYN	Welsh
EMRYS (EM-rees)	Welsh
EVAN	Welsh
EWAN, EWEN (Yoo-an)	Scottish
FARQUAR (FAR-kwar)	Scottish
FERGUS, FERGUSON	Scottish
FIFE, FYFE	Scottish
FORBES	Scottish
FRASER, FRAZIER	Scottish
GAEL (GA-el)	Breton
GAIR (Gar)	Scottish
GARETH	Welsh
GAWAIN (Gaw-an)	Cornish, Welsh
GERWYN (Ger-win)	Welsh
GLYN (Glin)	Welsh
GRAHAM	Scottish
GREGOR	Scottish
GRIFFITH	Welsh
GUTHRIE	Scottish
GWYNFOR	Welsh
HACO	Cornish
HAMISH (HAY-mish)	Scottish
IFOR (EE-for)	Welsh
INNIS (IN-ish)	Scottish
IOLO (YO-lo)	Welsh
JAGO (JAHG-o)	Cornish
JAKEZ (ZHAH-kays)	Breton

KADO (KAH-doh)	Breton
KEIR (Care)	Scottish
KELVIN	Scottish
KENDRICK	Scottish
KYLE	Scottish
KYNON	Welsh, Cornish
LENNOX	Scottish
LLEWELLYN	Welsh
MADOC (MAH-dog)	Welsh
MALCOLM	Scottish
MALO (MAH-loh)	Breton
MATH (MAHTH)	Welsh
MAXEN	Welsh
MELAN	Cornish, Breton
MELOR	Breton
MORAY	Scottish
MUNGO	Scottish
NYE (Nie)	Welsh
OGILVY	Scottish
ONILWYN (O-nil-win)	Welsh
PENWYN	Welsh
PETROC (Pet-rock)	Cornish
POL (POHL)	Breton
RHAIN (Rain)	Welsh
RHYDACH, RIDDOCK	
(Rid-ack, Rid-ock)	Cornish
RHYS, REESE (Rees)	Welsh

RUMO, RUMON	
(ROOM-o, ROOM-on)	Cornish
SAMZUN (SAHM-zoon)	Breton
SENAN (SENN-an)	Cornish
SIÂM (SHAM)	Welsh form of James
SIARL (SHARL)	Welsh form of Charles
SIÔN (SHON)	Welsh form of John
SIÔR (SHOR)	Welsh form of George
SULIAN, SULIEN (SIL-yen)	Breton, Welsh
TALIESIN (Tal-YES-in)	Welsh
TALWYN	Cornish
TANGUY, TANGI (TAHN-gee)	Breton
TARAN	Breton
TEILO (TAY-loh)	Welsh
TORIN	Cornish, Manx
TREMAINE, TREMAYNE	
(TRAY-main)	Cornish
TREVELYAN	Cornish
URIEN (Yoo-RI-un)	Welsh, Breton
VAUGHAN (VON)	Welsh
WYN, WYNN	Welsh
YANN (YAHN)	Breton

true

Ireland and the Irish may be cooler than anyplace or anyone, but let's face it: French clothes, Italian shoes, German art, American music, Russian supermodels—there's cool beyond the Irish Sea, too. In case you want to investigate cool *non*-Irish names for your baby, here are some choices in vogue throughout Europe and in the USA.

girls

ADDISON	ELIANA
ALESSIA	FEDERICA
ALLEGRA	FLAVIE
AMELIE	FLORA
ASHBY	FRANCESCA
CADENCE	GAIA
CLAUDIA	GIADA
COSIMA	GIANNA
DANICA	GINEVRA
EDEN	GIULIA

HARLOW

ILARIA

INDIGO

INÈS

IRIS

ISABELLA

JADA

LÉA

LENA

LETICIA

LILA

LOLA

LUCIA

LUDOVICA

LUNA

MANON

MARINE

MILEY

NATALYA

NEVAEH (*heaven* spelled backwards)

OCÉANE

OLIVE

PALOMA

PETRA

PIPER

POPPY

ROMY

RUBY

SADIE

SANNE

SAWYER

SOPHIE

TALLULAH

TATIANA

TRUE

VALENTINA

VIOLET

boys

ACE

ALEXEI

ANDREAS

AUGUST

BECKETT

CADEN

CLEMENS

COLE

CRUZ

DANE

ELIAS

ENZO

FABIAN

FELIX

FILIPPO

GULLIVER

HUDSON

ISAAC

JAGGER

KINGSTON

KRISTOF

LORENZO

LUCA

MADDOX

MAGNUS

MARCOS

MATEO

MAXIMILIAN

MILLER

NICO

ORION

ORSON

ROMEO

SEM

STONE

TANCREDI

THEO

TIBOR

WOLF

WYATT

either

ADRIAN

DAKOTA

JUSTICE

LUCA

MILAN

MISHA

PEYTON

PRESLEY

SASHA

SAWYER

TRUE

29

addisyn

Here, hot off the press from newspapers in Dublin and elsewhere across the country, are what Irish parents are choosing to name their newborns now:

girls

ABBI	ARABELLA
ADA	AVA
ADDISYN	BEATRICE
AILBHE (ALL-bay)	BERNADETTE
AISLING (ASH-ling)	BLÁTHNAID (Blaw-nid)
AISLINN (ASH-len)	CAMILLE
ALANNA	CAOIMHE (KEE-va)
ALICE	CARAGH (KAR-a)
AMELIA	CIANNA
AMELIE	CIARA (KEER-a)
ANNALIE	CLARA
AOIBHINN (EE-veen)	CLARE
AOIFE (EE-fa)	CLODAGH (KLO-da)

ÉABHA (AY-wa)

EITHNE (EN-ya)

ELAINA

ELIZA

EVA

EVIE

FAY

FIA

FIONA

GRACE

GRÁINNE (GRAWN-ya)

HARRIET

IONA

ISABEL/ISABELLE/ISOBEL

JULIET

LARAGH (La-ra)

LEEANNA

LIBBY

LILIAN

LUCIA

LUCY

LUDMILLA (Lud-ME-la)

LULU

MAEVE (Mayv)

MIA

MUIREANN (MWIRR-an)

NESSA

NIAMH (Neev)

NICOLA

NORA

OLIVE

OLIVIA

ORLA

ORLAITH (OR-lee)

PHILOMENA

RÓISÍN (Ro-SHEEN)

RUBY

SADHBH (Sive—rhymes with *five*)

SAMARA

SAOIRSE (SEER-sha)

SASHA

SIOBHAN (Shi-VAUN)

SIÙN (SHOON)

SOPHIE

SORCHA (SOR-ka or SOR-ra)

TAMSIN (TAM-zin)

TARA

THALIA

ZARAH

ZOE

boys

AIDAN

AILBHE (ALL-bay)

ALFIE	FREDDY
ARAN	GARETH
ARCHIE	GARVAN
BENEDICT	HARRY
CALEB	HARVEY
CALLUM	HUGH
CIAN (KEE-an)	HUGO
CILLIAN (KILL-ee-an)	ISAAC
CLEMENT	JACK
CONN	JARLATH (Jar-leth)
CONOR	JUDAH
CORMAC	JUDE
CUÁN (Koo-AWN)	KEALAN
DÁIRE (Da-ra)	KILLIAN
DECLAN (DEK-lan)	LEO
DIARMAID (DEER-mid)	LOCHLAN (LOK-lun)
DYLAN	LUKE
EAMON (Ay-mon)	MAX
EDDISON	MURROUGH (Mur-ah)
ÉNÁN (EE-nane)	NATHAN
EOIN (OH-in)	NED
FABIEN	NIALL (NEE-all)
FIACHRA (FEE-uk-rah)	NOEL
FINLAY	ODHRÁN (OH-ran)
FINN	OISIN (OH-sheen)
FIONN (FIN)	OSCAR
FLYNN	PADDY

PÁDRAIG (PAW-drig)

RIAN (REE-an)

RONAN

RORY

RUADHÁN (ROO-an)

SEAMUS (SHAY-mus)

SEBASTIAN

SENAN (SENN-an)

TADHG (TYEg)

THEO

TIARNÁN (TEER-nan)

TIERNAN

TOBY

cool cool

FAMOUS NAMES

cillian

COOL IRISH CELEB NAMES

There's no question that attachment to a celebrity—of the past or of the present—sprinkles a certain stardust on a name, and in our celebrity-driven culture, fame has become a more and more influential element in baby-naming. Some celebrity names are inspiring thousands of namesakes across various cultures—the glamorous Ava, for example, is now seen on popularity lists from Scotland to Scandinavia.

The following are inspirational Irish-named celebrities, mostly from the worlds of entertainment and literature.

AIDAN Quinn

AISLING (ASH-ling) O'Sullivan

BONO (b. Paul Hewson)

CIARÁN (KEER-an) Hinds

CILLIAN (KILL-ee-an) Murphy

CLODAGH (KLO-da) Rogers

COLIN Farrell

COLM (KUL-um) Meaney

COLUM (KUL-um) McCann

CONAN O'Brien

CORMAC McCarthy

DERMOT Mulroney

DERVLA Kirwan

EAMONN (Ay-mon) Campbell
    (The Dubliners)

ELVIS Costello (b. Declan McManus)

EMER (EE-mer) Martin

ENYA

EOIN (OH-in) Colfer

FEARGAL (FAR-gal) Lawler
(The Cranberries)

FEARGAL (FAR-gal) (b. Sean
Feargad) Sharkey

FERDIA MacAnna

FINOLA Hughes

FINTAN McKeown

FIONA Shaw

FIONNULA (Fin-OO-la) Flanagan

GAY (b. Gabriel, nickname
Gaybo) Byrne

LAOISE (LEE-sha) Kelly

LIAM Neeson

MAEVE Binchy

MALACHI (MAL-a-key) Cush

MALACHY (MAL-a-key)
McCourt

MILO O'Shea

NIALL (NEE-all) Toibin

NIAMH (Neev) Cusack

NOLAN Ryan

ORLA Fitzgerald

PADDY Casey

PÁDRAIC (PAW-ric) Delaney

PHELIM (FEY-lim) Drew

PIERCE Brosnan

REDMOND O'Hanlon

RODEN Noel

RÓISÍN (Ro-SHEEN) Murphy

ROMA Downey

RORY Gallagher

COOLEST
CELEB NAME
• • •
Saoirse

SAOIRSE (SEER-sha) Ronan

SEAMUS (SHAY-mus) Heaney

SINÉAD (Shin-AID) Cusack

SINÉAD (Shin-AID) O'Connor

SLÁINE (SLOYNE-ye) Kelly

SORCHA (SOR-ka or SOR-ra)
   Cusack

VAN Morrison

rafferty

Celebrities on both sides of the Atlantic, those with and without Hibernian roots, have long been partial to Irish names. Here are some of the coolest, along with our reasons for thinking so:

AIDAN • **Scott Hamilton (Olympic figure skater), Robert F. Kennedy Jr.**
Once a pet form of Aodh, which means "little fire," Aidan is spreading like wildfire from Edinburgh to Pittsburgh, prized for its strength and charm. Also seen as Aédán, Aodhán, Aiden, Eadan, and Edan.

AOIFE (EE-FA) • **Ciarán Hinds**
Popular name dating back to a fierce woman warrior in early myth, it has been anglicized as Eva and Ava.

BECKETT • **Malcolm McDowell, Melissa Etheridge, Conan O'Brien, Stella McCartney**
An appealing last-name name rich in literary associations, both to the play and film based on the life of Saint Thomas à B. and to

the Irish playwright-novelist Samuel B., it's red hot in Hollywood.

BRODY • Gabrielle Reece & Lance Hamilton

This superstar athlete couple's choice reflects the new trend toward using Irish surnames like Reagan/Regan and Riley for both sexes. This little Brody is a girl.

CAITLIN • Breckin Meyer

The pristine classic spelling of a name that's been exported, translated, and diluted into such phonetic forms as Katelyn and Kaitlyn.

CASHEL (KASH-IL) • Daniel Day-Lewis & Rebecca Miller

The Irish actor and his American wife chose an unusual Irish place name for their son; it's also seen as Caisel.

CIARÁN (KEER-AN) • Padraig Harrington

The golf star chose an authentic Irish name to match his own.

COLIN • Paul Stanley, Kevin James

The member of iconic ghoul rock group KISS picked this perennially popular offshoot of Nicholas, as did Kevin James.

CONNOR • Nicole Kidman & Tom Cruise

Spelled with one *n* or two, this anglicized version of Conchobar, renowned in Irish myth, has long been popular in Eire and is climbing the popularity lists of other countries as well.

DARBY • Patrick Dempsey

Disney's *Darby O'Gill and the Little People* made this spirited, lighthearted name seem more Irish than it actually is.

DELANEY • Martina McBride

A solid surname that's now used far more for girls than boys.

DONOVAN • Charisma Carpenter, Noel Gallagher

Another appealing surname, this one has long outgrown its "Mellow Yellow" associations.

FINLEY • Chris O'Donnell, Holly Marie Combs

One of the newly popular Fin-family of names, also spelled Finlay (as used by Sadie Frost).

FINN • Christy Turlington & Ed Burns, Jane Leeves

This is a name with enormous energy and charm, that of the greatest hero of Irish myth, Finn McCool. Other related cool star-baby names: FLYNN (Elle Macpherson) and FINNIGAN (Eric McCormack of *Will & Grace* fame), not to mention Julia Roberts's phabulous Phinnaeus.

FIONA • Jenny Garth

Although this name is a Scottish invention, it has an Irish feel and is commonly found among the Finolas and Fionnualas.

GULLIVER • Gary Oldman, Damian Lewis

This relatively rare Gaelic surname was known primarily through his literary *Travels* until actor Oldman transformed it into a lively baby-name option.

IRELAND • Kim Basinger & Alec Baldwin

If Ireland isn't Irish, what is?

JAMES PADRAIG (PAW-DRIG) • Colin Farrell

Cool combination of classic New Testament name with one of the many authentic versions of the name of Ireland's patron saint.

JUNO • Will Champion (Coldplay)

The success of the eponymous little-movie-that-could was sure to establish Juno, with its lively image and classic roots, as a potential baby name—and it's already started on its way.

KIERAN • Julianna Margulies

Irish *K* names are a hot commodity for boys—a category that includes Kieran, Keegan, Keaton, and Killian.

LENNON • Patsy Kensit & Liam Gallagher

Naming a child after your hero (cultural or otherwise) gives him two cool advantages: a name with real meaning and a positive image to reach toward. Another rocker, Zakk Wylde, chose Hendrix as his son's musical hero name.

LIAM • Calista Flockhart, Tori Spelling

Sprightly and richly textured classic that started as a short form of William.

MAEVE • Chris O'Donnell

An early Irish goddess and queen name, short but strong, now catching on across the pond. The O'Donnells named another of their five children Finley.

MALACHY (MAL-A-KEY) • Cillian Murphy

An Irish version of a biblical name, with an expansive, almost boisterous image.

MICHEAL • Liam Neeson & Natasha Richardson

The Northern Irish star stuck to the Gaelic spelling of the enduring Michael for his first son.

MILO • Ricki Lake, Camryn Manheim, Liv Tyler, Sherry Stringfield

Jaunty Irish spin on Miles, very popular with the glitterati.

OSCAR • Gillian Anderson, Hugh Jackman

This amiable Victorian favorite is having a definite revival among stylish parents on both sides of the Atlantic.

PADDY • Mare Winningham

Sure and it's one of the most enduring nickname names.

QUINLIN • Ben Stiller

A strong surname name usually spelled Quinlan that could make a child feel distinctive while still having the easy-to-handle nickname of Quinn.

QUINN • Sharon Stone

"The mighty Quinn" is a unisex name that's strong for both genders.

RAFFERTY • Sadie Frost & Jude Law

One of the coolest of the Irish surnames, with a raffish quality all its own.

REILLY • Roma Downey

There are Reillys and Rileys galore crossing both continental and gender lines.

RHIANNON (REE-A-NON)—Robert Rodriguez

The combination makes for an appealing cross-cultural mix. Some might consider it an improvement over the names of the director's four sons: Rebel, Rocket, Racer, and Rogue.

RILEY • David Lynch, Katie Wagner, Norah O'Donnell

See *Reilly*.

ROAN • Sharon Stone

A strong, red-haired choice.

RÓISÍN (RO-SHEEN) • Sinéad O'Connor

An authentic selection for a little Irish rose.

RONAN • Rebecca Miller & Daniel Day-Lewis

Compelling, legendary name of ten Celtic saints.

ROWAN • Brooke Shields

This friendly Irish surname was almost unheard of as a girl's name before Brooke Shields made the gender switch; now it shows lots of potential as a likable, unisex choice.

RYAN • Pete Sampras

Classic.

SAOIRSE RÓISÍN (SEER-SHA RO-SHEEN) • Courtney Kennedy

Meaning "liberty," Saoirse has been used since the 1920s as a statement of freedom.

SHEA • Kevin James

Common surname that projects spirit and substance; can also be seen as a short form of Seamus.

SULLIVAN • Patrick Dempsey

A jaunty Irish surname name with a real twinkle in its eye, used for the twin of brother Darby.

TALLULAH • Patrick Dempsey, Simon Le Bon, Philip Seymour Hoffman, Damon Dash, Demi Moore & Bruce Willis

The then Willises almost single-handedly launched the cool star-baby name concept when they chose SCOUT and RUMER as well as the more user-friendly Tallulah for their girls. This Anglicization of Tuilelaith is now being picked up on by other celeb parents.

And here are what some other Irish and Irish-American notables have chosen:

BONO • Jordan, Memphis Eve, John Abraham, Elijah Bob Patricus, Guggi Q

PIERCE BROSNAN • Sean, Dylan Thomas, Paris Beckett

ED BURNS • Grace (and Finn)

GABRIEL BYRNE • Jack Daniel, Romy Marion

DAVE (The Edge) EVANS • Hollie, Arun, Blue Angel, Sian

LIAM GALLAGHER • Gene, Molly (and Lennon)

NOEL GALLAGHER • Rory, Anais (and Donovan)

DENIS LEARY • Jack, Devin

DAMIEN LEITH • Jagger Ramone

JOEY MCINTYRE • Griffin Thomas

LIAM NEESON • Daniel Jack (and Micheal)

CONAN O'BRIEN • Neve (and Beckett)

KEVIN O'CONNOR • Brian Sean, Alexis Elaine, Colin Francis

SINÉAD O'CONNOR • Jake, Shane, Yeshua (and Róisín)

DOLORES O'RIORDAN • Taylor Baxter, Molly, Dakota Rain

PETER O'TOOLE • Kate, Patricia, Lorcan (LOR-kan)

AIDAN QUINN • Ava Eileen

STEPHEN REA • Danny, Oscar

COOLEST
STARBABY
NAME
• • •
Sullivan

phelim

COOL CHARACTER NAMES
FROM IRISH LIT

Here, some literary-inspiration suggestions coming from characters found in the pages of books spanning various periods of literary history. But in this category, as always, feel free to think about your own personal favorites.

female

CHARACTER	AUTHOR	BOOK
ADA	Anne Enright	*The Gathering*
AISLING		
(ASH-ling)	Maeve Binchy	*Light a Penny Candle*
AROON	Molly Keane	*Good Behaviour*
BABA (Bridget)	Edna O'Brien	*The Country Girls*
BRIDIE	William Trevor	*The Ballroom of Romance*
CAITHLEEN	Edna O'Brien	*The Country Girls*
CARMILLA	Sheridan Le Fanu	*Carmilla*
CATALINA	Edna O'Brien	*The High Road*

CIARA (KEER-a)	Colum McCann	*A Word in Edgewise*
EIBHLÍN (EV-lin)	Mícheál O'Guiheen	*A Pity Youth Does Not Last*
ELLENA	Richard Brinsley Sheridan	*The Critic*
EVERGREEN	Brian Cleeve	*Judith*
FIANNA (Fee-AHN-a)	Edna O'Brien	*The Heather Blazing*
HONOR	Iris Murdoch	*A Severed Head*
IMELDA	Roddy Doyle	*The Commitments*
IMOGEN	Aidan Higgins	*Langrishe Go Down*
ISOLT	Emer Martin	*Breakfast in Babylon*
ITA (Ee-ta)	Anne Enright	*The Gathering*
KAHEENA (Ka-HEEN-a)	Eoin Colfer	*Benny and Omar*
LETTY	William Trevor	*Reading Turgenev*
MARDA	Elizabeth Bowen	*The Last September*
MAURYA (Maur-ya)	Jennifer Johnston	*Old Jest*
MELODY	Roddy Doyle	*A Star Called Henry*
MINNIE	Christopher Nolan	*The Banyan Tree*
MOIRA (MOY-ra)	Colum McCann	*A Word in Edgewise*
NUALA (NOO-la)	Christopher Nolan	*The Banyan Tree*
ORNA	Eoin Colfer	*Benny and Omar*
PEIG (Peg)	Maurice O'Sullivan*	*Twenty Years a'Growing*
RAIN	Iris Murdoch	*The Sandcastle*

---

*also known as Muiris Ó Súilleabháin

SAOIRSE

    (SEER-sha)   Cecilia Ahern   *If You Could See Me Now*

male

CHARACTER	AUTHOR	BOOK
ARTEMIS	Eoin Colfer	*Artemis Fowl* series
BALTHAZAR	J. P. Donleavy	*The Beastly Beatitudes of Balthazar B.*
BEC	Darren Shan	*Bec*
CATO	Iris Murdoch	*Henry and Cato*
CHARLO	Roddy Doyle	*The Woman Who Walked into Doors*
DANBY	Iris Murdoch	*Bruno's Dream*
DECLAN	Colm Toíbín	*The Blackwater Lightship*
DECO	Roddy Doyle	*The Commitments*
DEKKO	William Trevor	*Beyond the Pale*
DORIAN	Oscar Wilde	*The Picture of Dorian Gray*
DOYLER	Jamie O'Neill	*At Swim, Two Boys*
EAMON (Ay-mon)	Edna O'Brien	*The Heather Blazing*
ENDA	Julia O'Faolain	*A Pot of Soothing Herbs*
EOIN (OH-in)	Colum McCann	*A Word in Edgewise*
HUGO	Iris Murdoch	*Under the Net*
IVOR	Anne Enright	*The Gathering*
JEM	Anne Enright	*The Gathering*
KIERAN	Colum McCann	*A Word in Edgewise*
LORCAN	Eoin Colfer	*Benny and Omar*

MALACHY		
(MAL-a-key)	Patrick McCabe	*The Dead School*
MICKAH	Roddy Doyle	*The Commitments*
MOR	Iris Murdoch	*The Sandcastle*
MOSS	Anne Enright	*The Gathering*
MUIRIS		
(Mwir-ish)	Micheál O'Guiheen	*A Pity Youth Does Not Last*
MYLES	John Banville	*The Sea*
NIALL (NEE-all)	Eoin Colfer	*Benny and Omar*
PÁDRAIG		
(PAW-drig)	Micheál O'Guiheen	*A Pity Youth Does Not Last*
PHELIM		
(FEY-lim)	Thomas Keneally	*Bring Larks and Heroes*
QUINTY	William Trevor	*My House in Umbria*
RONAN	Eoin Colfer	*Benny and Omar*
SEAGRUN		
(SHAY-groon)	Brian Cleeve	*Tread Softly in This Place*
SEBASTIAN	J. P. Donleavy	*The Ginger Man*
SWEENEY	Flann O'Brien	*At Swim-Two-Birds*
TALLIS	Iris Murdoch	*A Fairly Honourable Defeat*
TARRY	Patrick Kavanagh	*Tarry Flynn*
TOMÁS		
(To-MASS)	Maurice O'Sullivan*	*Twenty Years a'Growing*
VIRGILIUS	Sean O'Faolain	*The Man Who Invented Sin*

---

*also known as Muiris Ó Súilleabháin

xenia

NAMES FROM JAMES JOYCE

It's not easy to pluck names from the works of a writer who calls characters Gush and Roaring, Mutt and Butt. They range from the reasonably straightforward in *The Dubliners* to the somewhat riskier in *Ulysses* to the every-man-for-himself in *Finnegan's Wake*. Here are some of the more user friendly.

female

ADA	KATE
ANNA LIVIA	KATHLEEN
ANNIE	KITTY
BEATRICE	LILI
CELIA	LILY
DELIA	LISA
ELIZA	MARIA
EVELINE	MINA
GILLIA	MOLLY
IRIS	MORNA
JULIA	OLIVE

PHILOMENA   UNA (OO-na)

PHOEBE   WINNIE

POLLY   XENIA (ZEE-nee-a)

RUETIZZIE

JAMES JOYCE'S ABC'S

• • •

There's Ada, Bett, Celia, Delia, Ena, Fretta, Gilda, Hilda,
Ira, Jess, Katty, Lou (they make me cough as sure as I read
them), Mina, Nippa, Opsy, Poll, Queeniee, Ruth, Saucy,
Trix, Una, Vela, Wanda, Xenia, Yva, Zulma, Phoebe,
Thelma. And Mee!

—FINNEGAN'S WAKE

male

ALEXANDER   DUNBAR

ANDREW   FINN

BANTAM   GABRIEL

BARNEY   GARRETT

BARTELL   HUGH

BLAZES   IGNATIUS

BRIAN   KEVIN

CLIVE   LANTY

CONOLLY   LEO

DENIS   LEOPOLD

MALACHI (MAL-a-key)	**SEÁN/SHAUN**
MYLES	**SHEMUS**
NATHAN	**SIMON**
NED	**SMITH**
O'CONNOR	**STEPHEN**
PATRICK/PADDY/PATSY	**TERENCE/TERRY**
REUBEN	**VALENTINE**
ROCHE	**WISDOM**

GARDEN OF NAMES

• • •

Winnie, Olive and Beatrice, Nelly and Ida, Amy and Rue. Here they come, all the gay pack, for they are the florals, from foncey and pansey to papavere's blush, foresake-me-nought, while there's leaf there's hope, with primtim's ruse and marrymay's blossom, all the flowers of the ancelles' garden.

—FINNEGAN'S WAKE

juno

STAGE NAMES

Here, a menu of evocative names from the plays of four of Ireland's greatest playwrights, William Butler Yeats, George Bernard Shaw, Sean O'Casey, and J. M. Synge:

female

CHARACTER	PLAYWRIGHT	PLAY
AMARYLLIS	Shaw	*Back to Methuselah*
ARIADNE	Shaw	*Heartbreak House*
BRIDGET	Yeats	*The Land of Heart's Desire*
CANDIDA	Shaw	*Candida*
CATHLEEN	Yeats	*The Countess Cathleen*
	Synge	*Riders to the Sea*
CHLOE	Shaw	*Back to Methuselah*
DECIMA	Yeats	*The Player Queen*
DEIRDRE	Yeats	*Deirdre*
	Synge	*Deirdre of the Sorrows*
DELIA	Yeats	*Cathleen Ni Houlihan*

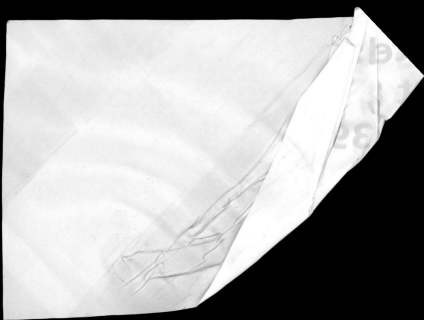

MALACHI (MAL-a-key)	SEÁN/SHAUN
MYLES	SHEMUS
NATHAN	SIMON
NED	SMITH
O'CONNOR	STEPHEN
PATRICK/PADDY/PATSY	TERENCE/TERRY
REUBEN	VALENTINE
ROCHE	WISDOM

GARDEN OF NAMES

• • •

Winnie, Olive and Beatrice, Nelly and Ida, Amy and Rue.
Here they come, all the gay pack, for they are the florals,
from foncey and pansey to papavere's blush, foresake-me-
nought, while there's leaf there's hope, with primtim's ruse
and marrymay's blossom, all the flowers of the ancelles'
garden.

—FINNEGAN'S WAKE

juno

STAGE NAMES

Here, a menu of evocative names from the plays of four of Ireland's greatest playwrights, William Butler Yeats, George Bernard Shaw, Sean O'Casey, and J. M. Synge:

female

CHARACTER	PLAYWRIGHT	PLAY
AMARYLLIS	Shaw	*Back to Methuselah*
ARIADNE	Shaw	*Heartbreak House*
BRIDGET	Yeats	*The Land of Heart's Desire*
CANDIDA	Shaw	*Candida*
CATHLEEN	Yeats	*The Countess Cathleen*
	Synge	*Riders to the Sea*
CHLOE	Shaw	*Back to Methuselah*
DECIMA	Yeats	*The Player Queen*
DEIRDRE	Yeats	*Deirdre*
	Synge	*Deirdre of the Sorrows*
DELIA	Yeats	*Cathleen Ni Houlihan*

EEADA (EE-ada)	O'Casey	*Red Roses for Me*
ELIZA	Shaw	*Pygmalion*
EMER (EE-mer)	Yeats	*The Only Jealousy of Emer*
EPIFANIA	Shaw	*The Millionairess*
FINNOOLA	O'Casey	*Red Roses for Me*
HONOR	Synge	*The Playboy of the Western World*
HYPATIA	Shaw	*Misalliance*
JUNO	O'Casey	*Juno and the Paycock*
LAVARCHAM	Synge	*Deirdre of the Sorrows*
LILITH	Shaw	*Back to Methuselah*
MAISIE	O'Casey	*Juno and the Paycock*
MAURTEEN	Yeats	*The Land of Heart's Desire*
MAURYA	Synge	*Riders to the Sea*
MINNIE	O'Casey	*The Shadow of a Gunman*
MOLLY	Synge	*The Well of the Saints*
NONA	Yeats	*The Player Queen*
NORA	O'Casey	*The Plough and the Stars*
	Synge	*Riders to the Sea*
OONA	Yeats	*The Countess Cathleen*
ORINTHIA	Shaw	*The Apple Cart*
PAUDEEN	Yeats	*The Unicorn from the Stars*
PEGEEN	Synge	*The Playboy of the Western World*
RAINA	Shaw	*Arms and the Man*
SIBBY	Yeats	*The Pot of Broth*
SOUHAIN (Soo-ann)	O'Casey	*Purple Dust*

male

ADOLPHUS	Shaw	*Major Barbara*
AINNLE		
(AWN-lya)	Synge	*Deirdre of the Sorrows*
ALEEL	Yeats	*The Countess Cathleen*
ARDAN	Synge	*Deirdre of the Sorrows*
AYAMONN		
(Eye-a-mon)	O'Casey	*Red Roses for Me*
BARTLEY	Synge	*Riders to the Sea*
CASHEL	Shaw	*The Admirable Bashville*
COLENSO	Shaw	*The Doctor's Dilemma*
CONCHUBOR		
(KON-er)	Synge	*Deirdre of the Sorrows*
CUTLER	Shaw	*The Doctor's Dilemma*
FERGIS	Synge	*Deirdre of the Sorrows*
FERGUS	Yeats	*Deirdre*
	Shaw	*You Never Can Tell*
FINCH	Shaw	*You Never Can Tell*
MAGNUS	Shaw	*Androcles and the Lion*
NAISI (NAY-see)	Synge	*Deirdre of the Sorrow*
NAOISE		
(NEE-sha)	Yeats	*Deirdre*
OCTAVIUS	Shaw	*Man and Superman*
OWEN	Synge	*Deirdre of the Sorrows*
PATRICK	Yeats	*Cathleen Ni Houlihan*
ROORY	O'Casey	*Red Roses for Me*

58

SERGIUS		
(Ser-gee-us)	Shaw	*Arms and the Man*
SEUMAS		
(SHAY-mus)	O'Casey	*The Shadow of a Gunman*
SHAWN	Synge	*The Playboy of the Western World*
	Yeats	*The Land of Heart's Desire*
SHEMUS	Yeats	*The Countess Cathleen*
TEIGUE (TYEg)	Yeats	*The Countess Cathleen*
VALENTINE	Shaw	*You Never Can Tell*
ZOZIM		
(SOS-eem)	Shaw	*Back to Methuselah*

finn

Name inspiration can come from almost anywhere, including your local movie screen. Here are some examples of Irish-named characters found in cinematic sources:

BERNADETTE	*The Wind That Shakes the Barley, Circle of Friends*
BRIDGET	*The Devil's Own*
CHRISTY (male)	*My Left Foot*
CONNOR	*Road to Perdition*
CONZO	*Goldfish Memory*
CRISPINA	*The Magdalene Sisters*
DAMIEN	*The Wind That Shakes the Barley*
DEIRDRE	*Intermission*
DERMOT	*Agnes Browne*
DONAL (DOH-nal)	*Conspiracy of Silence*
DUNCAN	*Con Air*
DYMPNA	*About Adam*

EAMON (Ay-mon)	*The Secret of Roan Inish*
FINBAR	*The Brothers McMullen*
FINN	*Road to Perdition*
FIONA	*The Secret of Roan Inish*
FLYNN	*The Secret of Roan Inish*
GARETH (female)	*In the Name of the Father*
GEMMA	*Cowboys and Angels*
HUBIE	*Tara Road*
ISOLDE	*Goldfish Memory*
LEHIFF (Lee-HIFF)	*Intermission*
LIAM	*Michael Collins*
MAISIE	*The Boys and Girl from County Clare*
MAJELLA	*Conspiracy of Silence*
MICHEAIL (Mee-HAL)	*The Wind That Shakes the Barley*
MIKO	*The Boys and Girl from County Clare*
NOELEEN	*Intermission*
PHELIM (FEY-lim)	*Rat*
RORY	*Rory O'Shea Was Here, The Devil's Own*
SADIE	*My Left Foot*
SEAN	*Circle of Friends*
SINÉAD (Shin-AID)	*The Wind That Shakes the Barley*

SIOBHAN

  (Shi-VAUN)   *Rory O'Shea Was Here*

TADGH (TYEg)   *The Field, The Secret of Roan Inish*

WHEELER   *Strength and Honor*

COOLEST
SCREEN NAME
• • •
Gareth for
a girl

orinthia

Writers everywhere sometimes feel constricted by the database of established names and feel moved to invent their own. Irish writers are no exception. The Northern Irish writer C. S. Lewis was perhaps the most inventive with names in his *Chronicles of Narnia,* which include the males Caspian, Rilian, Shasta, and Tirian. More often, however, writers concentrate their naming efforts on female characters. Here is a selection of girls' names that were the inspirations of Irish authors:

ANNA LIVIA
James Joyce drew this name from the ancient Irish name for the river Liffey: abha Lifi.

ARAVIS
An invention from C. S. Lewis's *Chronicles of Narnia*.

DAIREEN (DAUR-een)
Invented by Limerick author F. Frankfort Moore for the title character of his 1893 novel.

GLORIA

Conceived by George Bernard Shaw for the 1898 play *You Never Can Tell.*

GLORVINA

Invented name for a prince's daughter in Lady Morgan's *The Wild Irish Girl,* 1806.

MALVINA

In James Macpherson's Ossianic poems, Malvina was the invented name for the lover of Oscar, grandson of Finn McCool.

MAURYA

A character in J. M. Synge's 1904 drama, *Riders to the Sea.*

ORINTHIA

George Bernard Shaw created this name for his 1929 play, *The Apple Cart.*

VEVINA

Form of Bebhinn used in Ossianic poems.

ZAIRA (ZARE-ah)

Invented by the Irish writer C. R. Maturin for his novel, *Women; or pour et contre,* 1818.

THE WILD IRISH ROSES

American popular music has, from the mid-nineteenth century on, been a-burstin' with Irish songs. Either they waxed nostalgic for old Erin ("It's a Long Way to Tipperary," "Christmas in Killarney," "When Shall I See Ireland Again?" "Back to Donegal") or glorified dear sainted Mother ("That Old Irish Mother of Mine," "Ireland Must Be Heaven, for My Mother Came from There," "Mother Machree") or celebrated the Irish in general ("When Irish Eyes Are Smiling," "It's the Irish in Your Eye, It's the Irish in Your Smile"). But mostly they serenaded their sweethearts, some of whom were named as follows:

ANNIE Rooney	I'll Take You Home Again,
Sweet ANNIE Moore	KATHLEEN
JENNIE, the Flower of Kildare	KATHLEEN Mavourneen
JOSEPHINE, My JO	K-K-K-KATY
I Wish I Could Shimmy Like	Pretty KITTY Kelly
My Sister KATE	MAGGIE Murphy's Home

Since MAGGIE Dooley Learned the Hooley Hooley	PEG o' My Heart
MARY	PEGGY
Tip-Top Tipperary MARY	PEGGY O'Neil
Oh! What a Pal was MARY	ROSE of Killarney
MARY's a Grand Old Name	My Wild Irish ROSE
MOLLY O!	Dear Old ROSE
My Irish MOLLY O!	Sweet ROSIE O'Grady
Sweet MOLLY Malone	The Daughter of ROSIE O'Grady
NELLIE Kelly, I Love You	My Blushin' ROSIE

And the beat goes on. In more recent times, Irish colleens have continued to provide musical inspiration, for example:

BRENDA X	Poco
DEIRDRE	The Beach Boys
Come On, EILEEN	Dexy's Midnight Runners
KATHLEEN's Song	The Byrds
KATIE's Been Gone	The Band
Maybe KATIE	Barenaked Ladies
That's My KATIE	Tom Paxton
KATIE MAY	The Grateful Dead
KERRY	Hall & Oates
MAGGIE MAY	Rod Stewart, The Beatles
MAGGIE McGill	The Doors
MAGGIE's Farm	Bob Dylan
Along Comes MARY	The Association

MARY, MARY	The Monkees
MAUREEN	Sade
Good Golly, Miss MOLLY	Little Richard, Creedence Clearwater Revival
PEG	Steely Dan
PEGGY SUE	Buddy Holly, The Beach Boys, John Lennon
Pretty PEGGY-O	Bob Dylan
RHIANNON	Fleetwood Mac
Cracklin' ROSIE	Neil Diamond
Whole Lotta ROSIE	AC/DC
SHANNON	Henry Gross
SHEENA Is a Punk Rocker	The Ramones
SHEILA, Take a Bow	The Smiths
TARA	Roxy Music

pre-cool cool

OLD NAMES

emer

NAMES FROM IRISH MYTH & LEGEND

Ireland is rich in folktales and legends starring characters that range from pagan gods and goddesses to ancient kings and queens to the fairies who live in the roots of old trees. But perhaps the greatest Irish legends of them all center on the mythical hero Finn McCool, son of a slain warrior and a king's daughter, whose maternal grandfather tries to drown him the day he's born. The infant Finn McCool surfaces from his watery fate holding a salmon in his hand and is raised by his paternal grandmother in a cave with the dog Bran. He grows up to become a great warrior with mystical powers, derived from chewing his fingers, literally, to the bone. After using his magic to save the king's horse, Finn rejects the reward of the princess's hand in marriage and asks instead for the lives of the condemned champions of Erin. These champions become the followers of Finn, the first Fenians, or Fianna, of Ireland.

Many of the Irish names of myth that remain the most popular and appealing come from the Fenian legends. There's the princess Niamh, who ran away with Finn McCool's son, Ossian;

Grania, Finn's sweetheart, who eloped with Dermot; and Áine, who refused to sleep with any man but Finn. And on the male side, there are Dermot, Conan, Ossian, and of course, Finn Mc-Cool himself, the quintessential hero with the quintessentially cool name.

Some other names of Irish legend are likewise well-used in modern times: Deirdre, for instance, Eithne, Maeve, and Una for girls; Conor, Cormac, and Ronan for boys. And there are also names that survive only in legend that deserve to be revived: Caireann, Ceara, Dáire, and Glas are notable for their melodic qualities; while other names may inspire you because of their associations with mythical characters or events.

Still, many of the names that follow should perhaps stay confined to legend. It's difficult to imagine a modern child going through life with the name Blathnat, for example, or Abhartach.

Here, for inspiration or maybe just for edification, is a who's who of Irish myth and legend:

female

ACHALL (AH-hill)
Daughter of the legendary warrior Cairbre Nia Fer; she died of sorrow when her brother was killed.

AÍ (EYE)
Aí the Arrogant, daughter of Finn, who refused to marry any man who wasn't Irish. In keeping with her egotistical identity, her name is pronounced like the pronoun *I*.

AILBHE (ALL-bay)

One legendary Ailbhe was a daughter of the fairy king Midir; another was a daughter of Cormac mac Art and one of the four best lovers in Ireland.

ÁINE (AH-nya)

The name of many legendary heroines: a fairy queen; lover of the sea god who took her to the Land of Promise; daughter of the king of Scotland who would sleep with no man but Finn, whom she married and with whom she bore two sons.

AINNIR (AN-yir)

A character in the Finn tales.

ALMHA (AL-wa)

A member of the mythical tribe of divinities called the "people of the goddess Dana," the legendary ancestors of the Irish race.

AOIBHEALL (EE-val)

A pagan name of one of the ancient Irish goddesses. In various stories, she is the fairy who appears to Brian Boru on the eve of battle, the daughter of a warrior, and the daughter of a king of Munster.

AOIFE (EE-fa)

A warrior queen in love with Cúchulainn who bore him a son named Connla; the jealous stepmother in the Children of Lir tales.

(The name began to rise in popularity after Siamese twins named Aoife and Niamh were successfully separated in 1997.)

BÁINE (BAN-ah)
Daughter of the legendary ancestor of Ireland's kings.

BANBHA (BAN-va)
The name of an early Irish goddess who vied with sisters Fodla and Éire to have settlers name the country after them: obviously, Éire was the winner.

BEARACH (BAR-ak)
A character of legendary generosity, and the third wife of Finn.

BÉIBHINN (BAY-veen)
One legendary Béibhinn was daughter of the king of the Otherworld; another was the mother of the hero slain by Cúchulainn.

BINNE (BEE-ne)
Name of several fairy-women of Irish legend.

BLÁTHNAIT (BLAW-nid/BLA-na)
The wife of the Munster king Cú Roi and lover of Cúchulainn, whose life ended in tragedy; the word means "little flower."

BÓINN (BO-in)
Wife and mother of gods; goddess of the Boyne.

BRIGHID (Bridge-id)

A revered pagan goddess associated with poetry and fertility.

BUANANN (BOOAN-an)

A goddess; also a mother who tutored warriors in arms.

CAINNLEACH (KAN-lac)

Foster mother of an Ulster hero, she died of sorrow when her son was slain.

CAIRREAN (Kar-in)/CAIREANN

Daughter of the king of the Britons, mother of Niall of the Nine Hostages and legendary ancestress of the high kings of Ireland.

CATHACH (Ka-ha)

A legendary female warrior.

CIARA (KEER-a)

A wife of Nemed, a legendary invader of Ireland, who gave her name, Mac Cera to County Mayo.

CLÍODHNA (KLEE-oy-na)

The name of three mythical heroines: Tuatha Dé Danann, who gave her name to one of the three great waves of Ireland; one of the three beautiful daughters of Libra, poet to the sea god; and a fairy patroness to the MacCarthy clan.

CLOTHRA (KLOH-ra)

Sister of legendary queen Maeve.

COCHRANN (KAW-kran)

Mother of Dermot, the greatest lover in Irish legend, who eloped with Orania, Finn McCool's beloved.

CRÉD (KRAY-ed)

The name of several legendary queens and princesses, most notably the daughter of Cairbre, king of Ciarraige, who fell in love with the warrior Cáel and died of sorrow when he was slain in battle.

CRÓCHNAIT (KROHK-nitch)

Mother of the Fenian warriors Diarmait and Oscar.

DÁIRINE (Dar-EEN-a)

The daughter of a legendary king of Tara.

DANA

Pagan river goddess who bestowed her name on the Tuatha Dé Danaan, the legendary earliest inhabitants of Ireland.

DEIRDRE

Beautiful heroine of a tragic legend who was betrothed to the king of Ulster but eloped with the young warrior Naoise, who was then killed by the king, after which the grieving Deirdre threw herself out of a chariot and died.

DELLA

Came to Ireland in a legendary invasion led by Queen Cessair.

DOIREANN (DOR-an)

Daughter of the fairy king Midir.

DRAIGEN

Wife of the legendary ancestor of the kings of Munster.

DÚNLAITH (DOON-lee)

Daughter of the Connacht warrior Regamon; a popular name in the Middle Ages.

ÉABHA (AY-wa)

A wife of Nemed, legendary invader of Ireland; also, a Fenian heroine who was drowned at sea.

EACHNA (AK-na)

Daughter of a king, she was reputed to be one of most beautiful and intelligent women in the world.

EACHTACH (AK-ta)

A daughter of the great lovers Orania and Dermot.

ÉILE (EYE-la)

Sister of Queen Maeve.

ÉIRE (Ey-ra)

The victorious one of three sisters who competed to have Ireland named after her.

EITHNE (EN-ya)

One of the most popular names in Celtic legend, in particular of the beautiful and clever Eithne, or Ethniu, who was imprisoned in a crystal tower and bore Cian's child Lugh, god of the sun and of arts and crafts.

EMER (EE-mer)

Wife of the hero Cúchulainn who stoically endured his acts of un- faithfulness. Appreciated for her six gifts—of beauty, voice, sweet speech, needlework, wisdom, and chastity.

ÉRNE (AIR-n)

A princess after whom Lough Erne is named.

ÉTAÍN (Et-OIN)

One of several by this name who was considered "the most beautiful woman in all Ireland," but who, unfortunately, was turned by Midir's wife, Fuamnach, into a pool of water, a worm, and a fly.

ETAN (E-tain)

The name of Cúchulainn's mistress as well as of the daughter of the mythical god of healing.

EVEGREN (EVE-gran)

Daughter of the tragic Deirdre and Naoise.

EVLIN/EIBHLEANN (AYV-lan)

A mythical spirit who gave her name to a mountain range.

FAIFE (Fafe)

Daughter of Ailill and Queen Maeve.

FAÍLENN (FEE-len)

A princess and the mother of Eithne, wife of the king of Cashel.

FAINCHE (FINE-ke)

One name of the Irish goddess of war; also a mythical saint who, when threatened with marriage, jumped into Lough Erne and swam underwater to the sea.

FANN

Wife of the sea god.

FÉTHNAT (FAY-nat)

Musician to the Tuatha Dé Danann.

FIAL (Feel)

Wife of the founder of the O'Driscoll and O'Coffey families; also the name of Emer's sister and of a goddess.

FIDELMA (Fi-DEL-ma)/FEDELM

The name of several legendary queens, princesses, and great beauties.

FINNABAIR (Fin-ABAR)

A daughter of Queen Maeve and Ailill.

FINNCHÁEM (Fin-shame)

The wife of Cian, the mother of the hero Conall Kemach, or the daughter of one fairy king and the wife of another.

FINNCHNES (Finches)

In the Finn stories, the daughter of a king and also a robe maker for the Fianna.

FIONNUALA /FINNGUALA (Fin-GOO-la)

The daughter of the sea god Lir, who was turned into a swan by her jealous stepmother, Aoife, and cursed to wander the lakes and rivers of Ireland.

FLIDAIS (Fli-daze)

Daughter of Ailill Finn, the legendary Connacht king, she fell in love with an exiled warrior.

FODLA (Fo-la)

Wife of the god Mac Cecht whose name is another name for Ireland.

FUAMNACH (FOOM-na)

Wife of Midir, who in an act of jealousy turned her rival into a scarlet fly.

GRÁINNE (GRAWN-ya)/GRANIA

Finn McCool's betrothed, who eloped with Diarmait; together they hid in forests and caves for sixteen years in what's considered one of the greatest love stories of Irish legend.

GRIAN (Gray-an)

A daughter of Finn McCool, possibly the Irish sun goddess.

ISEULT (EE-soolt)

Irish princess who was the lover of Tristan in the tragic Arthurian legend.

IUCHRA (Oo-cra)

She turned Aoife, her rival, into a heron.

LÍADAN (LEE-dan)

Mother of Saint Ciaran who, according to legend, conceived him when a star fell in her mouth; a poet beloved by Cuirithir.

LÍBAN (LEE-von)

A mythical figure who lived beneath the sea for three hundred years.

LÚGACH (LOOG-a)

A daughter of Finn McCool.

MACHA (MOK-ah)

A war goddess of the Tuatha Dé Danann; another legendary Macha is called "Macha of the red hair."

MÁEN (Main)

Daughter of Conn of the Hundred Battles; another Máen was a king's daughter and mother of a legendary judge.

MAEVE /MEDHBN (Mayv)

The legendary Queen of Connacht who led an invasion of Ulster, which led to the death of Cúchulainn. The name means "she who intoxicates."

MARGA

Marga of the fairy mound was the mother of the beautiful but tragic Étain.

MELL

In Irish mythology, the mother of seven saints.

MUIREACHT (MEER-akt)

The wife of the king of Tara.

MUIREANN (MWIRR-an)

Occurs frequently in Irish mythology: as Oisín's wife, the foster mother of the hero Cáel and the wife of a king of Connacht.

MUIRÍN (MIR-in)

Lived for three hundred years in Lough Neagh.

MUIRNE (MWIR-neh)

The mother of the great warrior Finn McCool.

NEAMHAIN (Nee-OW-an)

An ancient war goddess.

NEASA (NASS-ah)/NESSA

The wily and ambitious mother of Conchobar, responsible for bringing him to the throne.

NIAMH (Neev)

Princess of the Land of Promise who left with Finn McCool's son Oisín for the Otherworld, where they lived happily for three hundred years.

ORLA (OR-la)/ORLAITH (OR-lee)

A name borne by both the sister and niece of Brian Boru.

SADHBH (Sive—rhymes with *five*)/SIVE

Beautiful daughter of Conn of the Hundred Battles and wife of the legendary Munster king Ailill. Another Sadhbh was the mythical mother of Oisín who was transformed into a deer by a sorcerer.

SAMHAOIR (SA-weir)
A daughter of Finn McCool.

SARAID (SOR-id)
Another daughter of Conn, who married to become a forebear of the royal Scots.

SÁRAIT (SOR-it)
A legendary ancestress of the people of Muskerry and of the kings of Scotland.

SCÁTHACH (SCAW-ha)
A female warrior and the teacher of Cúchulainn; another Scathach lulls Finn to sleep with magic music.

SCOTA (Scot-ah)
The name of two progenitors of the Irish race, the wife of Niul and the wife of Milesius.

SUANACH (SOON-a)
Sister of Finn McCool and mother of the warrior Fiachra.

TAILLTE (Tall-cha)
A mythical nurse; also the wife of Eochaidh, the last king of the aboriginals of Ireland.

TARA/TEAMHAIR (TAW-her)

A mythical character after whom the Hill of Tara is named.

ÚNA (OO-na)

Daughter of a legendary king of Lochlainn and the mother of Conn of the Hundred Battles.

male

AILBHE (ALL-bay)/AILBE

The name of twelve warriors of the Fianna. Another mythical Ailbhe went seeking the Land of Promise.

AILILL (AL-eel)

A warrior who fought a battle with the legendary Fothad, who had stolen his wife.

ÁINLE (AN-la)

An early sun god. Also, one of the three brothers who were slain by the king of Ulster, after he eloped with Deirdre.

AODH (EY)

This name appears frequently in Irish mythology and royal legend. One Aodh was a son of Lir, turned by Aoife into a swan.

AONGHUS (AING-gus)/AENGUS

Áengus of the Birds was the god of love and poetry among the pagan Irish.

BRAN

The name of two Fenian warriors as well as of Finn McCool's dog.

BREAS (Bras)

A popular name in myth and legend.

BRIÓN (BREE-on)

A name often found in very early legends, the most famous of which was the son of Echu mac Énna, ancestor of the O'Connors, O'Rourkes, O'Flahertys, O'Reillys, and other noble families.

CADHAN (KEE-an)

A legendary hero who, with his dog, killed a monster.

CÁEL (KAH-el)

A fallen Fenian hero, slain at the battle of Ventry.

CAIRBRE (KAR-breh)

There are two legendary Cairbres: one was the son of Cormac mac Art; another Cairbre was the son of Niall of the Nine Hostages, founder of a royal dynasty.

CASS

A legendary ancestor of the Dál Cais, from whom the families O'Brien, MacNamara, and O'Grady sprang.

CATHAIR (KAH-hir)

A legendary king of Leinster who had thirty-three sons.

CETHERN (KETH-ern)

A name for the god of the Otherworld; also father of a famous mythical Druid.

CIAN (KEE-an)

The name of several legendary heroes, including the son of the god of medicine, who became father to Lugh, the sun god, the father of Ulster warrior Cúchulainn.

CIONNAOLA (Kin-AY-la)

In early law legends, a hero who remembered every word he learned at law school and wrote it down to form the first written record of Irish law.

CLOTHACH (KLO-ha)

Grandson of Dagda, the Good God.

CONAIRE (KON-a-ra)

Name of a heroic high king, Conaire Már.

CONALL (KON-al)

The name of many legendary kings and heroes, including Conall Cernach, the great Ulster hero, and Conall Corc, founder of the kingship of Cashel.

CONÁN (KOH-nan)

Conán mac Mórna was a member of Finn McCool's warrior band.

CONN

The name of a legendary king, Conn of the Hundred Battles, who is supposed to have been an ancestor of many famous families, including the O'Neills, the O'Donnells, the O'Rourkes, the O'Dowds, and the O'Connors.

CONOR/CONCHOBAR (KON-er)

In an Irish epic, Conchobar macNessa was the king of Ulster.

CORMAC (KOR-mak)

Legendary king of Tara, Cormac mac Art, who was ancestor of the O'Neills.

CRIOFAN (KREE-fan)

The name of several legendary kings and warriors.

CÚCHULAINN/CÚ CHULAINN (KOO-KULL-in)

The greatest of all the Irish warriors, hero of the Irish epic, *The Cattle Raid of Cooley*.

CUMHAL (KOO-wal)

The father of Finn McCool, or MacCúmhail, Cumhal Mac Art was a king and champion of the west of Ireland, whose death in battle the day after his marriage was foretold by a druid.

DAGDA (DEI-da)

An imperial pagan god and leader of the legendary early inhabitants of Ireland.

DÁIRE (Da-ra)

An early fertility god.

DÁITHÍ (DA-hee)/DAHY

A nephew of Niall of the Nine Hostages and a king of Connacht.

DIARMAID (DEER-mid)/DERMOT

A hero of Irish legend who fell in love with Gráinne, the wife of Finn McCool. He had a mark on his face that made women fall madly, instantly in love with him.

DONN

The god of the dead.

ÉIBHEAR (EY-vir)

The son of Milesius; the name is an Irish version of the Latin Hibernia.

ÉNNAE (AY-nay)

A legendary king of Munster.

EOCHAIDH (YO-kee)

An extremely popular name in legend. One Eochaidh was a lover of the fairy Étain.

FAERGHUS (FAHR-gus)/FERGUS

Fergus mac Róich was one of the heroes of the epic *The Cattle Raid of Cooley,* famed for his strength and stamina; Fergus mac Erca, legendary leader of the Gaels' migration from Ireland to Scotland in the fifth century.

FEDELMID (Fe-DEL-mid)
The name of several mythological heroes, including the ancestor of the O'Neills.

FIACHNA (FAKE-na)
The son of a mythical sea god and brother of Fionnuala.

FIONN (Fin)/FINN
Finn McCool or Fionn mac Cúmhail, the greatest legendary hero of them all: leader of the Fianna, a band of thousands of warriors, musicians, poets, priests, and physicians; acquired the gift of wisdom by touching the Salmon of Knowledge and sucking his thumb when he burned it cooking the fish; was the father of the master poet Oisín; spurned lover of Gráinne.

FÍTHEL (Fee-thel)
A legendary judge; also, a brother of Finn.

FRÁECH (Frake)
The son of a fairy-woman, said to be the handsomest man in all Ireland and Scotland.

GAEL (Gale)
Hero for whom the Irish race is named.

GLAS

Glas Mac Aonchearda, a Fenian and follower of Finn McCool.

INSIN

The foster son of Finn McCool who was killed by the Greeks while defending Finn against them.

LABHRAIDH (Lau-ree)

Labhraidh of the Red Hand was a Fenian hero who traveled with Oscar.

LÓCH (Lohk)

A mythological ancestor of the kings of Munster.

LUGH (Loo)

Son of the goddess Eithne, known as "master of all the arts."

MIACH (Me-ak)

A skilled craftsman, son of the pagan god Diancecht.

MIDIR (Mid-EER)

Fairy son of the god Dagda and lover of the beautiful Étain.

MORANN

A legendary judge of ancient Ireland who supposedly never gave an unjust verdict; also ten Fenian warriors.

MOROLT (MOR-olt)

Brother of Iseult, Tristan's doomed lover.

NAOISE (NEE-sha)

Deirdre's tragic lover.

NUADU (Noo-A-doo)

God of the Otherworld; the fisher-god.

OISÍN/OSSIAN (OH-sheen)

The son of Finn McCool, he was the poet of the Fiana. He was married to Éibhir, but still managed to have a three-hundred-year alliance with Niamh Chinn Óir.

OSCAR

Finn McCool's grandson, one of the great warriors of the Fianna.

COOLEST
HERO NAME
• • •
Cian

africa

NAMES OF IRISH KINGS & QUEENS

Until the twelfth century, when the Norman invaders finally got a stronghold in Ireland and the English king Henry II declared himself the country's overlord, Ireland was ruled by high kings as well as by a number of provincial kings and queens. The names of the most notable kings and queens—Brian Boru, Rory O'Connor, Gráinne O'Malley, and the ancient queen Aoife, to name just a few—remain well used to this day. But there are many more ancient royal possibilities that are more obscure, and perhaps even cooler.

If raising a little Irish prince or princess is what you have in mind, look to this list for naming inspiration:

female

ABHLACH (Av-lah)
An Ulster princess and mother of a king.

AFRICA
Daughter of Fergus of Galway, who married Olaus the Swarthy, King of the Isle of Man.

AILBHE (ALL-bay)/ELVA

Daughter of a high king and mother of a warrior-king.

AILIONORA (A-lee-o-NOR-a)/ELEANORA

Popularized by two queen consorts of England and introduced to Ireland by the Normans, the name was borne by several noble-women.

AILLEANN (ALL-yan)

Two kings' mothers bore this name.

ÁLMATH (AL-math)

An early Ulster princess.

AOIBHINN (EE-veen)/EAVAN

The name of several princesses, including a daughter of the royal prince of Tara who died in the tenth century.

AOIFE (EE-fa)

Daughter of King Dermot of Leinster who married Strongbow, leader of the Norman invasion; also the name of many other princesses.

AURNIA (Our-NEE-a)

Wife of Turlogh More O'Brien, thirteenth-century king.

BAILLGHEAL (Bwill-YALL)

A pious queen of Connacht.

BAIRRIONN (BAR-in)

Wife of a twelfth-century Ulster king.

BEBHAILL (BAY-vill)

Queen of the high king Donnchad mac Aeda.

BÉIBHINN (BAY-veen)/BEVIN

Wife of Tadgh, tenth-century king of Connacht.

CAINNECH (KAN-ya)

Tenth-century princess.

CAOINTIARN (KEEN-cheern)

Two wives of high kings.

CEALLACH (KAL-uk)

Eighth-century princess. More common as a male name; gave rise to the last name O'Kelly.

CLODAGH (KLO-da)

The name of a river popularized as a first name when the marquis of Waterford gave it to his daughter.

COWLEY/COBHLAITH (KO-lee)

A daughter of the powerful king Cano; also an eighth-century Leinster princess.

CRÉD (KRAY-ed)

The name of several Irish queens and princesses, as well as of the mistress of Cano.

CRINOC (Krin-oc)

An eleventh-century Munster princess.

DAMHNAIT (DAV-nit)/DAVNIT

Wife of a king of Munster and ancestress of the O'Moriartys, O'Cahills, O'Flynns, and O'Carrolls.

DEARBHÁIL (DER-vil)/DERVAL

The name of several medieval queens and princesses.

DERVOGILLA (Der-vo-gila)

The wife of Tiernan O'Rourke, king of Breifne; she eloped with Dermot McMurrough, king of Leinster, but later repented and became a nun.

DOIREANN (DUR-an)/DORREN

The mother of Gilla Patraic, an eleventh-century king.

DÚNLAITH (DOON-lee)/DUNLA

Wife of the high king Niall Frassach as well as the name of daughters of two high kings.

EACHRA (AK-ra)

A tenth-century princess noted for her beautiful complexion.

EIBHLÍN (EV-lin)

A popular aristocratic name in Northern Ireland. It was brought to Ireland by the Normans in the forms Avelina and Emeline; is identical with the English Evelina and Evelyn; and—while it achieved popularity as Eibhlin—it has been retranslated as Eileen, Aileen, and other variations.

EITHNE (EN-ya)

The name of several early queens and princesses.

FAÍLENN (FEE-len)

An early Cashel princess.

FINNEACHT (Fin-ahkt)

A princess of Meath and the mother of a saint.

FLANN

The name of two famous early queens.

FORLAITH (Forla)/FARVILA

A princess who became an abbess.

GORMLAITH (Gorm-lee)

The name of several early and well-known queens, including the wife of high king Brian Boru, who was also a daughter of the king of Leinster and the mother of Sitric, king of Dublin.

GRÁINNE (GRAWN-ya)/GRANIA
Gráinne Mhaoel Ni Mhaolmhaigh, or Grace O'Malley, was the sixteenth-century queen of the Western Isles who is a poetic symbol of Ireland.

LASSAR (Lasare)
An early princess.

LÍOCH (LEE-ahk)
The daughter of one high king and wife of another.

MAOL MHUADH (Mail-WOOEY)
The name of several wives and daughters of kings and high kings.

MÓR (More)
The name of several queens of Ireland, and one of the most popular medieval names.

MUIRGHEAL (Mwir-ial)
The name of at least several queens of Ireland.

NÁRBHLA (NAHR-vla)/NARVLA
The daughter of a prince and the wife of an abbot.

RANALT (RAN-alt)
Daughter of Awley O'Farrell, king of Conmacne, and wife of Hugh O'Connor, twelfth-century king of Connaught.

RÓNAIT (Ron-it)
The daughter of a high king.

SADHBH (Sive—rhymes with *five*)/SIVE
Daughter of Brian Bam.

SÉADACH (SHAY-da)
An eleventh-century princess.

TAILLTE (Tall-cha)
Daughter of the king of Meath and wife of High King Turlough O'Connor.

TEMAIR (TAY-mar)/TARA
The wife of a seventh-century high king.

TUATHLA (TOO-la)
An early queen of Leinster.

UALLACH (Ool-ach)
Chief poetess of Ireland in the tenth century.

male

AILILL (AL-eel)
Ailill Molt, an early king.

AINMIRE (AHN-meer-a)
Sixth-century king of Tara.

AODH (EY)/HUGH
The name of many kings and nobles, including three high priests.

ART
Art McMurrough, medieval king of Leinster.

AWLEY (AW-lee)
Awley O'Farrell, king of Conmacne.

BÁODÁN (Bway-DAWN)
The name of two powerful sixth-century kings.

BLATHMACC (BLAW-vak)
A seventh-century king of Tara.

BRANDUBH (BRAN-duh)/BRANDUFF
A medieval king of Leinster.

BREASAL (Bras-al)
An early Leinster king.

BRIAN/BRIÓN (BREE-on)

Name of the most famous high king of Ireland, Brian Boru, who defeated the Norse.

CAILLÍN (KAL-een)

An early prince who was ancestor to a dynasty of Cork kings.

CALLAGHAN (KAL-a-han)

A tenth-century king of Munster.

CANO (KAN-o)

A seventh-century king of Scotland and Ireland.

CATHAL (Kah-hal)

The name of a thirteenth-century king of Connacht, Cathal Crobhlhearg.

CEARÚL (KAR-ool)

The name of a great warrior-king and of many noblemen of Leinster.

CEAT (KAT)

King of Corcumroe; pronounced *Cat*.

CINÁED (Kin-AY-ad)

An eighth-century high king.

CONALL (KON-al)

Conall Cernach was a great Ulster hero.

CONCHOBAR (KON-er)/CONOR

Conchobar mac Nessa was king of Ulster.

CONGAL (KON-gal)/CONNELL

A seventh-century Ulster king and an eighth-century high king.

CORMAC (KOR-mak)

Cormac MacCuilleanan, bishop and king of Munster. Also the name of several other kings, as well as the legendary ancestors of the O'Neills, O'Briens, and MacNamaras.

CRÍONÁN (Kree-NAWN)

An eleventh-century king and an ancestor of the O'Falveys.

CRUINN (Krin)

An early king of Ulaid and the founder of a dynasty.

CUÁN (Koo-AWN)

An early king; also an eleventh-century poet.

CUANA (Koo-AN-a)

An early warrior and the king of Fermoy.

DÁITHÍ (DA-hee)/DAHY

A king of Tara.

DALLÁN (Dal-AWN)

Two famous early poets.

DEÁMAN (Dya-MAUN)

An early Ulster king.

DIARMAID (DEER-mid)/DERMOT

Dermot MacMurrough, the twelfth-century Leinster king, who invited the Normans into Ireland.

DÓNAL (DOH-nal)

The name of five high kings.

DONNCHADH (Donn-ca)/DONAGH (Dun-ah)

High King Donagh, son of Brian Boru.

DÚNLANG (DOON-lang)

The name of two early kings, one who was an ancestor of the O'Donoghues and another who was an ancestor of the O'Tooles and O'Byrnes.

FAOLÁN (FAY-lan)

The name of three kings of Leinster between the seventh and ninth centuries.

FELIM (FEY-lim)

A medieval king of Connacht.

FERGUS

The name of several early kings.

FINGUINE (Fing-wine)

The name of two early Munster kings.

FLAITHRÍ (FLAH-ree)

An early king; also an archbishop of Tuam and a distinguished ecclesiastic and writer.

FLANN

A distinguished name borne by a king, a high king, who was an ancestor of the O'Connors, and several famous early poets.

GLASSÁN (Glas-AWN)

An early Ulster prince.

GORMAN

A king of Munster and an ancestor of the O'Keefes.

GUAIRE (Goo-ARA)

A king of Connacht famed for his generosity.

KENNEDY

King Kennedy of Munster, father of Brian Boru.

KENNELLY

The principal poet of Munster.

LACHTNA (LOKT-na)/LUCIUS

The name of several early kings and nobles, including the brother and the great-grandfather of Brian Boru.

LAOGHAIRE (LEE-ra)/LEARY

A king of Tara.

LENNÁN

An early king.

LORCÁN

The name of several kings, including the grandfather of Brian Boru.

MAHON

Brian Boru's brother and a tenth-century king of Cashel.

MALACHY (MAL-a-key)

The name of two famous high kings of Ireland.

MUIRÍOS (Mwir-EE-us)

A favorite name among noble Connacht families.

MURTAGH (MUR-tah)

The name of three kings of Tara, as well as of the prince called Muircheartach of the Leather Cloak.

NIALL (NEE-all)

King of Tara, Niall of the Nine Hostages, who founded the Uí Néill dynasty of Irish kings; also Niall Black-Knee, founder of the O'Neill family, who died fighting the Norse in the tenth century.

RUAIRÍ/RORY

Rory O'Conor, who ruled 1166–70, was the last high king of Ireland. Rory O'Donnell was the last king and first earl of Tyrconnell.

RUMANN (ROOM-an)

A great early poet.

SHANE

An Elizabethan-era Irish prince, Shane the Proud, who was chief of the O'Neill family.

SITRIC

The name of several kings of Dublin in the Middle Ages, most notably Sitric Silkenbeard.

SUIBNE (SIV-nee)/SWEENEY

An early high king.

TADGH (TYEg)

The name of several ancient kings and princes, including the son of Brian Boru, spelled Tadc.

TIBBOT

The son of Grania or Grace O'Malley, Tibbot of the Ship was so called because he was born at sea.

TURLOUGH (Tur-loch)

The name of two kings, Turlough I O'Brien and Turlough II O'Conor, who ruled in the tenth and eleventh centuries.

redmond

IRISH HEROES & HEROINES

Not all the Irish heroes and heroines are ancient ones. More modern heroes—political, ethical, or artistic—might inspire a young namesake.

AUGUSTA

Augusta, Lady Gregory, early-twentieth-century writer and dramatist, was a co-founder of the Abbey Theatre and a champion of the revival of the Irish language and ancient folklore.

CATHAL

Cathal Brugha was an Irish Civil War patriot and founder of the Republic.

COLLINS

A founder of the Irish Republican Army, Michael Collins negotiated the controversial treaty that gave Ireland dominion status within the British Empire. He was assassinated in 1922.

CONNOLLY

James Connolly was a Socialist Party leader who was instrumental in the 1916 Easter Rebellion, for which he was executed.

CONSTANCE

Constance Georgine Gore-Booth became Countess Markiewicz, a heroine of the Easter Rebellion. She was the only woman sentenced for her role in the revolt and became an early government leader of the Irish Republic.

ÉAMON

Éamon de Valera, president of Ireland from 1959 to 1973, played a key role in the emergence of the republic.

EMMET

Robert Emmet, the great Irish orator and patriot, led an unsuccessful revolt against the British in 1798. Sentenced to die in 1803, he said, "When my country takes her place among the nations of the earth, then, and not till then, let my epitaph be written."

EOGHAN

Pronounced as Owen, Irish patriot Eoghan Roe "Red Eoghan" O'Neill triumphed over the British in the 1646 battle at Benburb.

HUGH

Two heroic Hughs—Hugh O'Neill, earl of Tyrone, and Red Hugh O'Donnell, earl of Tyrconnell—joined forces to lead a rebellion and defeat the forces of the British Queen Elizabeth I.

MAUD

Yeats's muse, actress and activist Maud Gonne founded the Daughters of Ireland, a women's republican movement, at the turn of the last century. She was instrumental in many relief efforts during the Irish Civil War.

O'CONNELL

Last name as first in honor of Daniel O'Connell, early nineteenth-century lawyer who campaigned for Catholic emancipation and was known as the Liberator.

OLIVER

Oliver Cromwell's slaughter of one-quarter of the Irish Catholic population in the 1650s, and his subsequent sale of many Irish into West Indian slavery, might have permanently turned the Irish (who despise Cromwell to this day) against the name Oliver were it not for the saving grace of Saint Oliver Plunkett, an Irish archbishop who was executed by the British in 1681. If not for the saintly Oliver, naming a little McKenna or Connelly Oliver would have been as unthinkable as calling a baby Greenberg Adolf.

PEARSE

Padraig Henry Pearse was an Irish poet and patriot killed after the Easter Rebellion.

REDMOND

Popular in Northern Ireland, Redmond O'Hanlon (there's also a modern travel writer with this name) was an Irish "Robin Hood" who lived during the Cromwellian era. John Redmond was a Parliamentarian whose support for Britain during World War I made him unpopular with revolutionaries but has won the favor of moderates.

ROBINSON

If we can have Robinson Crusoe, why not name your child after the first woman president of Ireland, Mary Robinson?

RÓISÍN

Róisín Dubh is the heroine of an 1835 poem that reflects an Irish tradition of hiding outlawed patriotic sentiments within a love song.

SAOIRSE

The Irish word *saoirse*—pronounced SEER-SHA and meaning "freedom" or "liberty"—has been used since the 1920s and symbolizes patriotism.

SHANE

In the sixteenth century, Shane O'Neill led armies that were victorious over Elizabeth I.

TURLOUGH

Turlough Carolan was a blind, itinerant harper who lived from 1670 to 1738 and is considered Ireland's national composer.

WOLFE

Wolfe Tone, who lived at the end of the eighteenth century, is considered the father of the Irish Republican movement. Initially devoted to trying to bring about reform by uniting Protestants and Catholics, Tone became convinced that armed rebellion was the only route to Irish freedom.

tallula

SAINTS PRESERVE US!

There are hundreds and hundreds of Irish saints—so many, in fact, that it seems as if every second person walking about the land in the fifth, sixth, and seventh centuries must have been beatified. Not so surprising when you consider that Ireland was a center of religious learning and fervor in those days, and sainthoods were also more generously conferred. And although many of their names live on only through the religious notoriety of their most famous bearers and are otherwise obsolete, there is a sizable group that are lovely and still appealing possibilities for twenty-first-century children. Here is a list of what we consider the coolest and most usable choices:

girls

NAME	OTHER/MODERN FORMS
ÁINE (AH-nya)	*ANYA, ENYA*
AODHNAIT (EY-nitch)	*ENIT* (Een-it), *ENA* (AY-na), *ENY* (Any)

ATTRACTA

BLÁTH (BLAW) — *FLORA*

BLINNE (BLIN-ya) — *MONINNE* (Mon-EEN)

BREACNAIT
(BRACK-nitch) — *BRECCNAT* (Brek-nat)

BRÍGH(Bree) — *BRIG, BREE*

BRIGID — *BRIDGET, BRID* (Breedge),
BREDA (BREE-DA)

CAOILFHIONN
(KALE-in) — *KEELIN*

CAOIMHE (KEE-va) — *KEEVA*

CIAR (Keer) — *CIARA* (KEER-a), *KIARA*

CIARA (KEER-a) — *CERA* (KER-a), *KEIRA*

CLOTHACH (KLO-ha) — *CLORA*

CONNA

DÁIRE (Da-ra) — *DARYA* (DAH-ree-a), *DARY*

DAMHNAIT (DAV-nit) — *DYMPHNA* (Dimf-na)

DANA

DEARLÚ (JAR-loo)

DYMPHNA (Dimf-na)

ÉADAOIN (Ay-deen) — *AIDEEN*

EITHNE (EN-ya) — *ENYA, ETNA*

FAINCHE (FINE-ke) — *FANCHEA* (Fansha)

FAOILEANN (FAY-lan) — *FAILENN* (FEE-len)

FIDELMA (Fi-DEL-ma)

FIONNAIT (FYAN-it) — *FIONA*

ÍDE (EED-eh) — *EDA, IDA*

NAME	OTHER/MODERN FORMS
INA (Eena)	
ITA (Ee-ta)	
LÍADAN (LEE-dan)	*LELIA*
LONÁN (Lo-NAUN)	*LONAN*
MEADGHBH (MEEV)	*MAEVE* (Mayv)
MUADHNAIT (MOON-itch)	*MONA, MONAT* (Mon-at)
NÉAMH (NEYV)	*NEVE* (Neev), *NÉM* (Name)
ÓRNAIT (OR-nit)	*ORNA*
RÍONACH (REE-nah)	*RINA* (Reena)
SCIATH (SKI-ya)	*SKIA* (Ski-a)
TALULLA	
TARA	
TEAMHAIR (TAW-her)	*TARA*
TUILELAITH (TOO-lee)	*TALLULA*

boys

NAME	OTHER/MODERN FORMS
ABÁN (*Ah-BAWN*)	*ABBÁN* (Ah-BAWN)
AENGUS	*ANGUS*
AILILL (AL-eel)	*AILBE* (ALL-bay)
AODH (EY)	*ÁED, HUGH*
AODHÁN (EY-gaun)	*AIDAN*
AONGHUS (AING-gus)	*AENGUS, ANGUS*
BEAGÁN (Bug-AWN)	*BECCÁN* (Bek-awn)
BRAN	

BRAON (Brain)	
BREACÁN (BRAK-an)	*BRECCÁN* (BREK-an)
BRENDAN	
BRÓGÁN	*BROGAN*
CAOIMHÍN (KEEV-een)	*KEVIN*
CASS	
CIANÁN (KEE-nan)	*KEENAN*
CIARÁN (KEER-an)	*KIERAN*
CILLÍN (Kill-EEN)	*CILLIAN* (KILL-ee-an), *KILIAN*
COILEÁN (Kill-AWN)	*COLIN*
COLM (KUL-um)	*CALAM* (Kal-am),
	COLUMB (KUL-lum)
COLMÁN	*COLMAN*
CONALL (KON-al)	*CONAL* (KON-al), *CONNELL*
CONÁN	*CONAN*
CONLAODH	*CONLEY*
CORCÁN (Kor-KAWN)	*CORCCÁN*
CORCRÁN (Kor-KRAWN)	*CORCORAN* (KOR-kran)
CORMAC	
CRÍOFÁN (KREE-fan)	*GRIFFIN*
CRÓNÁN (KROH-NAWN)	*CRONAN*
CUÁN (Koo-AWN)	
DÁIRE (Da-ra)	*DARY*
DALLÁN (Dal-AWN)	
DAMHÁN (Dav-AWN)	*DAMAN* (DA-man), *DAVAN,*
	DAVIN
DEAGLÁN (DEG-laun)	*DECLAN* (DEK-lan)

DIARMAID (DEER-mid)	*DERMOT* (Der-mut)
DÓNAL (DOH-nal)	
DONNÁN (Don-AWN)	
DUFACH (DUFF-ock)	*DUFFY*
EARNÁN (AR-naun)	*ERNAN*
ELÁIR (AY-lair)	*ALAIR*
EOGHAN (OH-ah)	*EOIN* (OH-in), OWEN
EOLANN (YO-lan)	*OLAN*
EVIN	*EVAN*
FAIRCHEALLACH (FAR-ka-la)	*FARRELLY*
FAITHLEANN (FIE-lan)	*FALLON*
FAOLÁN (FAY-lan)	*PHELAN* (FAY-lan)
FEARGHUS (FAR-us)	*FERGUS*
FINBARR	
FINNÉN (Fin-EYN)	*FINIAN*
FINTAN/FIONNTAN (FIN-tan)	
FIONNÁN (Fin-AWN)	*FINNÁN* (FIN-awn)
FLANN	
FLANNÁN (Flan-awn)	*FLANNAN*
GARBHÁN (GAR-vawn)	*GARVIN*
IODHAR (Yo-ver)	*IBOR* (EE-bor), *IVOR* (EE-vor)
ÍOMHAR (Yo-war)	*IVOR* (EE-vor), *IFOR* (EE-for)
LAOIRE (LAY-re)	*LEARY*
LORCÁN (LOR-kaun)	*LORCAN* (LOR-kan)
LUCAN (LOO-kan)	

117

LUGHÁN (LOO-awn)	*LUGÁN*
MAC DARA	*MACDARRA*
MAOL EOIN (Mail-own)	*MALONE*
MAOL MHUIRE (Mail-were)	*MURRAY, MYLES*
MAOLMHAODHÓG (Mail-MEY-oh)	*MALACHY* (MAL-a-key)
MEALLÁN (MEHL-lahn)	*MELLÁN* (Mel-AWN), *MALLON*
NAOMHÁN (Nay-VAUN)	*NEVAN*
OISÍN (OH-sheen)	*OSSIAN*
ÓRÁN (OH-ran)	*ORAN*
PÁDRAIG (PAW-drig)	*PÁDRAIC* (PAW-ric) , *PATRICK*
RÍAN (REE-an)	*RIAN, RYAN*
RODÁN (RO-dan)	*RODAN*
RÓNÁN (RO-nan)	*RONAN*
RÚADHÁN (ROO-an)	*ROWAN* (RO-an)
SEANÁN (Shah-NAUN)	*SENAN*
SIOLLÁN (Shil-AWN)	*SILLÁN* (Sil-AWN)
TADHG (TYEg)	*TADE, TEAGUE*
TIARNACH (TEER-nok)	*TIERNEY*
TIARNÁN (TEER-nan)	*TIERNAN*
TRESSAN	*TRESIAN*

HOLIER BY THE DOZEN

To multiply further the number of Irish saints, there are several names that count more than one saint to their credit. A lot more than one, if ancient Irish records can be believed, for there are the following numbers of saints with these names:

COLMÁN (KUL-mawn): 234

FINTAN/FIONNTAN (FIN-tan): 74

MOCHUA (Mu-KOO-a): 59

MOLAISSE (MO-lass): 46

MO LUA (Mu-LOO-a): 38

MOCHUMA (Mu-KOOM-a): 33

COLUM (KUL-um): 32

CIARÁN (KEER-an): 26

AIDAN/AODHAN: 21

AODH (EY)/HUGH: 20

BRÉNAINN (BRAY-nan)/ BRENDAN: 17

BRIGIT: 15

FAOLÁN (FAY-lan): 14

BRECCÁN (BREK-an)/BREACÁN (BRAK-an): 13

BRÍGH (Bree): 13

COOLEST
SAINT'S NAME
• • •
Lorcan

lugh

THE CELTICIZER

In their search for a cool-sounding Irish name, some parents have begun to reverse the trend of anglicizing traditional Gaelic names by going back to the originals or creating their own Irish-ish versions of Anglo names. Thus, if you wanted to honor your Grandpa Arnold, and couldn't find a direct Irish coordinate, you might fudge it by using something like Ardgal or Ardál instead. Here are some examples, but again, do feel free to improvise.

girls

ANGELA	AINGEAL (ANG-gil)
CHARLOTTE	SÉARLAIT (SHAR-lit)
CLARE	CLÁR (Klawr)
CLAUDIA	CLODAGH (KLO-da)
EDNA	EITHNE (EN-ya)
EILEEN	EIBHLÍN (EV-lin)
EVELYN	AOIBHINN (EE-veen)
FRANCES	FAINCHE (FINE-ke)
GERTRUDE	GRANIA (GRAWN-ya)

GLORIA	GIOLLA
HELENA	LÉANA (Lee-AN-a)
ISABEL	ISIBÉAL (Is-a-BEL)
LOUISE	LABHAOISE (Loo-EE-sha)
MABEL	MÁIBLE (MAY-bla)
MARGERY	MAILSI (MOLL-she)
MOLLY	MAILLE (MOLL-ye)
PATRICIA	PÁDRAIGÍN (PAUD-rig-een)
PAULINE	PÓILÍN (PO-leen)
POLLY	PAILI (PAHL-ee)
RACHEL	RÁICHÉAL (RAYTCH-el)
SARAH	SARAID (SOR-id)
SHEILA	SÍLE (SHEE-la)

boys

ALAN	AILÍN (EY-lin)
ALBERT	AÍLBE or AILBHE (ALL-bay)
ARNOLD	ARDÁL (AHR-dal)
AUSTIN	OISTIN (OSH-teen)
BASIL	BREASAL (Bras-al)
BERNARD	BEARACH (BAR-ak)
CALVIN	CEALLACHAN (KAL-uh-han), CALBHACH (KAL-wa), CALVAGH (KAHL-va)
CARY	CARRAIG (Korr-ig)
CONRAD	CONRÍ (KON-ree)
DUDLEY	DUBHDARA (Doov-DOR-ra)

EARL	AEL (AII-eel)
EUGENE	EOGHAN (OH-in), EUNAN (YOU-nan)
EZRA	EOCHO (YO-ko)
GERALD	JARLATH
HAROLD	ARALT (Ar-ahlt)
KEVIN	CAVAN (KAV-an)
LARRY	LAOIRE (LAY-re)
LEW	LUGH (Loo)
MARK	MARCÁN (MOR-kawn)
MARTIN	MÁIRTIN (MAUR-teen), MARTÁN (Mar-TAUN)
PETER	PEADAR (PAH-der)
RAYMOND	RÉAMONN (RAY-mon)
RONALD	RÓNAL (RON-nal)
STEPHEN	STIOFÁN (Sti-FAWN)
STEVEN	STÉBHÍN (STAY-veen)
THEODORE	THADÓIR (Tha-dor)
VINCENT	UINSEANN (IN-sun)
WALTER	UALTAR (WAL-tar)

maguire

FAMILY NAMES

If you want a cool name from your family tree—but you can't find any from recent generations for easy plucking—consider these choices traditionally used in various clans.

The good news is you can look back through names associated with all the various branches of your family to find some original and unexpected ideas. Don't forget too that families often dropped the prefixes *Mac, Mc,* and *O'* over time, so if your family name is Kelly, you might consider O'Kelly family favorites Grania and Malachy as your own.

The bad news is that there are many more names for boys here than for girls. Male names were more often passed down through a family, and also were more likely to be recorded, whereas female ones are often lost to time. And many of these family names are, shall we say, a tad eccentric. Your heart may soar to spot your last name O'Madden on this list, only to feel it sink when you discover your family names are Breasal and Coganus. Such oddities may make better middle names than firsts. Some traditional names may be better left in the family graveyard. Awley Magawley? We don't think so.

We include both the Irish Gaelic and Anglicized forms of a name when both were used; when only one version is recorded, that's the one we include.

girls

LAST NAME	FIRST NAME
Lowther	JANA
MacDermott	DERBHAÍL (DER-vel)/DERVAL
	FIONNUALA (Fin-OO-la)/FINOLA
	LASAIRIONA (Loh-ser-EEN-a)/
	LASRINA (Loh-SREEN-a)
MacDonagh	LASAIRIONA (Loh-ser-EEN-a)/
	LASRINA (Loh-SREEN-a)
MacMahon	BENVY
MacNamara	SLÁINE (SLOYNE-ye)
MacNamee	GRÁINNE (GRAWN-ya)/GRANIA
McCourt	AISLINN (ASH-len)
O'Beirne	LASAIRIONA (Loh-ser-EEN-a)/
	LASRINA (Loh-SREEN-a)
O'Brien	CAOIMHINN (KEEV-een)
	FIONNUALA (Fin-OO-la)/
	FINOLA
	SLÁINE (SLOYNE-ye)

O'Connor	**BENVY**
	ÉTAOIN (AY-deen)
	FIONNUALA (Fin-OO-la)/
	FINOLA
O'Duffy	**GRÁINNE (GRAWN-ya)/GRANIA**
O'Flannagan	**ÉTAOIN (AY-deen)**
O'Gormley	**GRÁINNE (GRAWN-ya)/GRANIA**
O'Hanley	**LASAIRIONA (Loh-ser-EEN-a/**
	LASRINA (Loh-SREEN-a)
O'Hara	**ÉTAOIN (AY-deen)**
O'Kane	**AISLINN (ASH-len)**
	RÓS (RO-ish)
O'Kelly	**GRÁINNE (GRAWN-ya)/GRANIA**
O'Murray	**RÓIS (Roh-ish)**
O'Neill	**BENVY**
Wallis	**EDITHA**

boys

LAST NAME	FIRST NAME
Barrett	**TOIMILIN (Tom-il-in)**
Barry	**DOWLE (Dow-il)**
Bradley	**AIBHNE (AV-nya)/EVENY**
	(EV-nee)
Brady	**MAZIERE (Ma-ZEER)**
Brody	**AIBHNE (AV-nya)/EVENY**
	(EV-nee)

Burke	FIACHA (FEE-uk-ah)/FESTUS
	UILLEAG (ILL-ag)
	UILLIAM (UHL-yam)
Campbell	COLIN
Clibborn	ABRAM
Fitzgerald	GARRET
Glenny	ISAAC
Joyce	GILL
Kavanagh	ART
	CRIOFAN (KREE-fan)/ GRIFFIN
	MURCHADH (MUR-kah)/ MORGAN
MacAlister	AONGHUS (AING-gus)/AENEUS (Ay-EE-nee-us)
MacArdle	MALACHY (MAL-a-key)
	RÉAMONN (RAY-mon)/ REDMOND
MacBrannon	CONN
MacCabe	AIRDGAL (Ard-gal)
MacCann	LOCHLAINN (LOK-lun)
	MALACHY (MAL-a-key)
	RÉAMONN (RAY-mon)/ REDMOND
	RUAIDRÍ/RORY
MacCarthy	CEALLACHAN (KAL-uh-han)/ CALLAHAN

	DIARMAID (DEER-mid)/
	DERMOT (Der-mut)
	FININ/FLORENCE
	JUSTIN
MacClancy	BOETIUS
MacCloskey	MÁNUS (MAU-noos)
MacCormack	AONGHUS (AING-gus)/AENEUS
	(Ay-EE-nee-us)
MacCoughlin	ROSS
MacDermott	MAOLRUANÍ (Mail ROON-ee)/
	MYLES
MacDonagh	BRIAN
MacDonnell	AONGHUS (AING-gus)/AENEUS
	(Ay-EE-nee-us)
	ALASTAR
	COLLA (KULL-a)
	FEARADHACH (FEER-ga)/
	FREDERICK
	RANDAL
	RUAIRÍ/RORY
	SORLEY
MacDowell	ALASTAR
MacEgan	BEOLAGH (Bee-OH-la)
	LUKE
MacElligot	UILLEAG (ILL-ag)/ELIAS
MacFaden	MANUS
MacGillespie	TARLACH (TAHR-lok)/CHARLES

MacGovern	BRIAN
	TIARNÁN (TEER-nan)
MacKenna	LOCHLAINN (LOK-lun)
MacKiernan	ART
	DUARCAN (DOOR-kan)/
	DURKAN
	TIARNÁN (TEER-nan)
Macken	RÉAMONN (RAY-mon)/
	REDMOND
MacLoughlin	MUIRCHEARTACH (Mur-CAR-ta)/
	MURTAGH (MUR-tah)
	OSCAR
MacMahon	AIRDGAL (Ard-gal)
	BRIAN
	GLAISNE (GLASH-na)
	IRIAL (IRR-yal)
	ROSS
MacMasterson	DUARCAN (DOOR-kan)/
	DURKAN
MacMurrough	ART
MacNamara	CUMHEA (KOO-va)
	MACCON (Mack-on)
	SHEEDY
MacNarnee	FARRELL
	LOCHLAINN (LOK-lun)
	SOLAM (SO-lam)/SOLOMON
MacNicholl	MANUS

MacSweeney	TARLACH (TAHR-lok)/CHARLES
	DUBHGHALL
	(DOO-gall)/DOUGAL
	ÉIREAMHÓN (ER-ev-one)/IRWIN
	EOGHAN (OH-in)
Magawley	AWLEY (AW-lee)
Magennis	ÉIBHEAR (AY-vir)
	GLAISNE (GLASH-na)
Maguire	DONN
	OSCAR
	PILIB
	ROSS
Malone	LOCHLAINN (LOK-lun)
McGinley	RUAIRÍ/RORY
McRory	AIRDIN (Ar-deen)
Mulloy	RUAIRÍ/RORY
Nugent	BALTHASAR
O'Boyle	DUBHGHALL (DOO-gall)/
	DOUGAL
	FARRELL
O'Breslin	TARLACH (TAHR-lok) /CHARLES
O'Brien	ANLUAN (AN-loo-an)/ANLON
	AINMIRE (An-MEER-eh)/
	ANVIRRE (AN-virr-eh)
	BRAN
	CONCHOBAR (KON-er)/
	CONNOR

	DIARMAID (DEER-mid)/
	DERMOT (Der-mut)
	DONNCHADH
	(Donn-ca)/DONAGH (Dun-ah)
	KENNEDY
	LAOISEACH (LEE-sha)/
	LUCIUS
	MUCHADH (Moo-koo)/
	MURROUGH
	TARLACH (TAHR-lok)/
	TERENCE
O'Brody	DÁIRE (Da-ra)
O'Byrne	FIACHA (FEE-uk-ah)
	GARRETT-MICHAEL
	UGHAIRE (Oo-JAR-a)
O'Carroll	MAOLRUADHAN (Mal-ROO-ahn)/
	MULRONEY
O'Clerkin	FARRELL
O'Clery	CONAIRE (KON-a-ra)
	LUGHAIDH (Loo-EE)/LEWIS
	TUATHAL (TOO-hal)/TULLY
O'Connell	MUIRGHEAS (Muir-yas)/
	MAURICE
	MURCHADH (MUR-kah)/
	MORGAN
O'Connelly	AIRDGAL (Ard-gal)
O'Connor	ART

	BRIAN
	CALBHACH (KAL-wa)/CHARLES
	CONCHOBAR (KON-er)/
	CONNOR
	DIARMAID (DEER-mid)/
	DERMOT
	EOGHAN (OH-in)/OWEN
	FAILGHE (Fail-ga)
	MACBEATHA (Mak-BA-ha)/
	MACBETH
	OSCAR
	RUAIDRÍ/RODERICK
	TOMALTACH (Tom-AL-ta)/
	THOMAS
O'Daly	BAOLACH (BWAY-la)/BOWES
O'Dempsey	FINN
O'Dempster	FAILGHE (Fail-ga)
O'Doherty	CONALL (KON-al)
	RUAIRÍ/RORY
	TOIMILIN (Tom-il-in)
O'Donnell	AINEISLIS (An-EYSH-lish)
	AODH (EY)/HUGH
	CATHBHARR (KAH-war)/
	CAFFAR
	CONALL (KON-al)
	CONN
	EOGHAN (OH-in)

	MANUS
	NECHTAN (Nek-tan)
	NIALL (NEE-all)/NEILL
	RUAIRÍ/RORY
O'Donoghue	AMHLAOIBH (Ow-lee)/AULIFFE
	SEAFRA (SHAY-fra)/GEOFFREY
O'Donovan	AINEISLIS (An-EYSH-lish)
	MURCHADH (MUR-kah)/
	MORGAN
O'Dowd	TOMÁS (To-MASS)
O'Driscoll	FINN
	MACCON (MACK-on)
O'Dunne	FAILGHE (Fail-ga)
O'Falvey	DONNCUAN (Don-COON)
O'Farrell	CEADACH (KAID-uck)/KEDAGH
	FACHTNA (FOKT-na)/FESTUS
	IRIAL (IRR-yal)
	ROSS
O'Flaherty	MAONACH (MAIN-ah)
O'Flanagan	MALACHY (MAL-a-key)
O'Flynn	CU ULA (Koo-ul-a)/CULLEN
O'Gallagher	CONALL (KON-al)
	TARLACH (TAHR-lok)/
	CHARLES
	TUATHAL (TOO-hal)/TULLY
O'Gormley	SORLEY
O'Grady	STANDISH

O'Halloran	ÉIREAMHÓN(ER-ev-one)/ EREVAN
O'Hanlon	RÉAMONN (RAY-mon)/ REDMOND
O'Hanly	BEARACH (BAR-ak)/BARRY
O'Hara	AILILL (AL-eel)/OLIVER
	CIAN (KEE-an)/KEAN
	DUARCAN (DOOR-kan)/ DURKAN
O'Herlihy	CEALLACHAN (KAL-uh-han)/ CALLAHAN
O'Higgins	TUATHAL (TOO-hal)/TULLY
O'Hogan	CRONEY
O'Kane	AIBHNE (AV-nya)/EVENY (EV-nee)
	ECHLIN (Ek-lin)
	JARMY
	MANUS
O'Keeffe	CORC
	FINGUINE (FIN-een)
	GORMAN
O'Kelly	BREASAL (Bras-al)
	BRINE
	FERADACH (Fer-da)
	FIACHRA (FEE-uk-rah)/FESTUS
	LOCHLAINN (LOK-lun)/ LAURENCE

	MALACHY (MAL-a-key)
	NIALL (NEE-all)/NEILL
	UILLIAM (UHL-yam)
O'Kennedy	DONN
O'Lafferty	ÉIBHEAR (AY-vir)
O'Loughlin	IRIAL (IRR-yal)
O'Madden	ANAMCHA (AN-am-ha)/
	AMBROSE
	BREASAL (Bras-al)
	COFACH (Ko-fa)
O'Mahoney	CIAN (KEE-an)/CAIN
	FININ
	MAOL MHUIRE (Mail-were)/
	MOLLOY (Mo-LOY)
O'Mara	ELAN (AY-lan)
O'Meeha	MOLAISSE (Me-LISS-a)/
	LAZARUS
O'Molloy	UAITNHNE (Oo-ee-neh)/
	GREENE
	CEADACH (KAID-uk)/KEDAGH
O'More	CONMHAC (KON-wak)/CANOC
	FACHTNA (FOKT-na)/FESTUS
	RUAIDRI/ROGER
O'Morgan	MALACHY (MAL-a-key)
O'Moriarty	CORC
	SEANCHEN
	(SHAN-ken)/JONATHAN

O'Mullin	AIBHNE (AV-nya)/EVENY (EV-nee)
O'Mulloy	ART
O'Neill	CONN
	ENRI
O'Nolan	UGHAIRE (Oo-JAR-a)
O'Quinn	NIALL (NEE-all)/NEILL
O'Reilly	GLAISNE (GLASH-na)
	MYLES
O'Rourke	ART
	CONN
	FEARGHAL (Far-gal)/FARRELL
	TIARNÁN (TEER-nan)
O'Shaughnessy	RUAIDRI/ROGER
O'Sullivan	BUADACH (BOO-ahk)/ BOETHIUS
	FININ
O'Toole	BARNABY
	DONNCUAN (Don-COON)
	GILKEVIN
	LORCAN
Parsons	SAVAGE
Reynolds	IOR (EE-or)
Trant	ION (EE-on)
Wall	UILLEAG (ILL-ag)/ELIAS
Ward	MANUS

flann

BLONDS, BRUNETTES, & ESPECIALLY REDHEADS

An ever-growing segment of parents subscribe to the belief that you shouldn't name a child until you see what he or she looks like. A number of traditional Irish names fit in with this notion, meaning "fair" or "dark" or "red-haired." The catch, of course, is that a baby's coloring at birth may differ considerably from what it will be a year—or ten or twenty—down the road.

Many of the earliest Irish names connote dark coloring or dark hair—perhaps a hint that the Gaels who arrived around the time of Christ came from Spain. Fair coloring was more unusual among the early Irish, and so more prized, with mythical and heavenly creatures often described as having golden hair. The Vikings, who invaded Ireland in the ninth and tenth centuries, made blond and red hair more common.

You may want to consider one of these colorful choices for your own little blond, brunette, or redhead.

NAMES FOR DARK-HAIRED BABIES

girls

BARRDHUBH
  (Bar-uv)/BARDUFF

BRENNA

CAREY

CIAR (KEER)

CIARA/KEARA/KIERA/KIRA
  (KEER-a)

CIARNAIT (KEER-nit)

DUIBHEASA (Div-as-a)/
  DUVESSA

DUÍNSEACH (Doin-sha)

DÚNLAITH (DOON-lee)/
  DONLA

KERRY

ORNA

boys

BRANDUBH (Bran-duv)/
  BRANDUFF

CIARÁN (KEER-an)/KIERAN

CIARMHAC (KEER-voc)

CRÓNÁN (KROH-NAWN)/
  CRONAN

DOLAN

DONAHUE

DONEGAN

DONLEAVY

DONNABHAN (DUNN-a-vaun)/
  DONOVAN

DONNAGÁN (DUNN-
  a-gaun)/DONAGAN

DONNÁN (Don-AWN)

DONNCHADH (Donn-ca)/
  DONAGH (Dun-ah)

DONOVAN

DOUGAL

DOYLE

DUALTACH (Doo-al-thok)/
  DUALD (DOO-ald)

DUBH (Duv)/DUFF

DUBHAGÁN (DUGG-an)

DUBHÁN (DOO-an)/DUANE

FEARDORCHA (Fahr-dor-eka)/
  FARRY

KERWIN

SULLIVAN

TEIMHNÍN (Tev-NEEN)/
  TYNAN

DARCY

DELANEY

DONNELLY

DUFFY

GORMÁN

NAMES FOR FAIR-HAIRED BABIES

girls

BÁINE (BAN-ah)

BÉIBHINN (BEH-vin)/
  BEVIN

CAOILAINN (KALE-in)/
  KEELIN

CEALLACH (KAL-uk)/
  KELLY

CÉIBHIONN (KAY-vin)

FINNÉADAN (Finn-AY-dan)

FINNSEACH (Fin-sha)

FIONA

FIONNUALA (Fin-OO-la)/
  FINOLA

FIONNÚIR (Fin-OOR)

MUIREANN (MWIRR-an)/
  MUIRINN (MIR-in)

MUIRGHEAL (Mwir-ial)/
  MURIEL

NIAMH (Neev)

NUALA (NOO-la)

UAINIONN (OO-an-in)

boys

CAOIMHÍN (KEE-veen)/KEEVIN

FINN

FINNBARR

FINNEGAN

FINNIAN

FINTAN

LACHTNA (LOKT-na)

ORAN

either

AILBHE (ALL-bay)/ALBY

ALBANY

BAIRRFHIONN (BAR-fin)/
  BARRY

MOINGIONN (Mun-gan)

NAMES FOR RED-HAIRED BABIES

girls

COCHRANN

CORCAIR (KOR-kar)

FLANNAIT (Fla-nitch)

RÓISÍN (Ro-SHEEN)

SCARLETT

boys

ALROY

CORC

CORCÁN

CORCRÁN/CORCORAN

DEARGÁN (JAR-gan)

FLANNÁN (Flan-AWN)

LOCHLAINN* (LOK-lun)

either

CLANCY

DERRY

FLANN

FLANAGAN

FLANNERY

FLYNN

RUAIRÍ/RORY

ROWAN

---

*Though this name does not strictly mean "red-haired," it's a nod to the "land of the lochs," homeland of the Vikings, who brought fair and red hair to Ireland.

new cool

CREATIVE NAMES

donegal

COOL IRISH PLACE NAMES

From Tipperary to Tralee, Irish place names are melodic and evocative. Some of the selections on this list may strike you as thoroughly feminine, others strongly masculine, but most, we think, could work well for children of either sex.

Names of Irish towns, countries, rivers, and hills, both real and imaginary, that have been or could be used for both boys' and girls' first names include these:

ADARE	BALLINA
ARAN	BARROW
ARBOE	BOHO
ARDAGH (AHR-da)	BOYLE
ARDARA	BOYNE
ARDNAREA (Ard-NAR-eea)	BRAY
ARLESS	CARLOW
ARMAGH (Ar-MA)	CARRA
ATHY	CARRICK
BALLA	CARY

CASHEL	GYLEEN
CASHEN	IERNE (I-yearn)
CAVAN	INISHEER (In-is-eer)
CLARE	JUVERNA (You-VER-na)
CLAREEN	KAVANAGH
CLIFDEN	KERRY
CLODAGH (KLO-da)	KILCLARE
CLOONE	KILDARE
CONNEMARA (Kon-a-MAHR-a)	KILKENNY
CONNOR	KILLALA (Kill-A-la)
CORBALLY (Kor-bal-EE)	KILLEIGH (Kill-AY)
CULLEN	KILLIAN
CURRAGH (KURR-a)	KINSALE
DERRY	LEENANE (Lee-NANE)
DONEGAL	LEIGHLIN (LAY-lin)
DOON	LIFFEY
DUBLIN	LOUGHLIN (LUK-lin)
DUFFERIN	LUCAN
DULANE (Do-lin)	MAHEE (Ma-HEE)
DURROW	MALLOW
EALGA (Al-ga)	MANULLA
EMLY	MAYO
ENNIS	MEADE
FINN	MONAGHAN
FINNEA (FIN-ay)	NAVAN
GALWAY	OMAGH (OH-mah)
GLIN	OOLA

PALLAS	SUTTON
QUIN	TARA
RAHAN	TEMPO
RAMOAN	TIAQUIN (Tee-a-kin)
ROSS	TORY
SAMHAOIR (Sam-eer)	TRALEE (Tra-LEE)
SCOTA	TULLA
SHANDON	TYRELLA
SHANNON	TYRONE
SLANE	VALENTIA
SLIGO (SLY-go)	VARTRY
SUIR (Soor)	WICKLOW

COOLEST
PLACE NAME
• • •
Oola

lennon

Last names used as first names are in general hip, but Irish family names—and the Irish were among the first cultures to use more than one name—have a special blend of spirit and tradition that has made them particularly adaptable as first names, used all over the English-speaking world. We're all familiar with Ryan and Kelly, Casey and Clancy, Barry and Blake, but there are countless others waiting to be discovered and switched into first position. Here are a few ideas, with an element of their coolness, but by all means, feel free to comb through the branches of your own family tree.

BAILEY

Spreading like wildfire through the USA as a first name for both boys and girls, and a starbaby fave.

BAKER

Occupational last-name names are a hot new category, and this is one of the most appealing.

BANNAN

A name connected to one of the most famous haunted castles in Ireland.

BEHAN

A literary name strongly associated with acclaimed playwright Brendan Behan.

BOYLAN

A fourteenth-century poet praised the Boylans for their horsemanship and blue eyes.

BRENNAN

A more modern-sounding spin on the traditional favorite Brendan.

CALLAGHAN/CALLAHAN

Could be a twin name with Kelly, as they both derive from Ceallach.

CASSIDY

Took on an enduring cowboy image via TV and movie Western icons Hopalong and Butch Cassidy.

CLOONEY/CLUNY

Meaning "grassy meadow" or "sexy international superstar."

CONNERY

Strongly associated with the super-suave James Bond, Scottish-born Sean Connery.

CONNOLY/CONOLLY

A Donegal lawyer named William Conolly (1662–1729) was, in his day, reputed to be the richest man in Ireland.

CONROY

A distinguished Irish last name connected for generations with hereditary poets and chroniclers to the kings of Connacht.

CONWAY

Notable Conways have included eminent religious, military, and scientific figures—plus one country-western star.

COONEY

It comes from the Irish *cuanna,* which means "handsome" or "elegant."

CORRIGAN

The family motto is "Wisdom and impetuosity"—a cool combination. Downside: the phrase Wrong-Way Corrigan.

CREA (KRAY)

Can be used on its own, or as its paternal ancestor, McCrea.

CROSBY

Gained international fame via nonchalant midcentury crooner Bing Crosby, followed up by Crosby, Stills, and Nash.

CULLEN

Ireland's first cardinal was Cardinal Paul Cullen of County Kildare.

CURRAN

Unusual and savory name, conjuring up images of curry and currants.

DEEGAN

A very old name meaning "son of the black-haired one."

DENNISON

A cooler namesake for Grandad Dennis.

DOLAN

Fresh choice to replace Dylan or Nolan.

DONNELLY

Has lots of rhythmic three-syllable energy.

DONOGHUE/DONAHUE

Brian Boru, the most famous of the high kings, had a son with this name.

DUFFY

Slightly rowdy feel, would be right at home in a noisy pub.

DUGAN

Open, friendly, and cheerful.

EGAN

Its likeness to the word *eager* gives Egan a ready-to-please, effervescent energy.

FINNEGAN

Tied to one of the great works of Irish literature, James Joyce's *Finnegan's Wake,* already used by one celeb—*Will & Grace*'s Eric McCormack—for his son.

FLAHERTY

A name borne by several early Irish kings.

FLANAGAN

Has a warm, cozy, flannelly feel.

FLYNN

Like Flann and Flanagan, suited to a redhead.

GALLAGHER

Good for a future traveler, as it means "lover of foreigners."

GILLIGAN

Cool despite connection to dorky TV character.

HOGAN

Cool first-name possibility, à la Scottish Logan.

KAVANAGH/CAVANAGH

A substantial surname that moves beyond Casey and Cassidy.

KEENAN

In the Middle Ages, the Keenans were distinguished clergymen and historians; it's been the first name of three ancient saints and one Wayans brother.

KENNELLY

A contemporary-feeling namesake for an ancestral Kenneth.

LANIGAN

Found mostly in Kilkenny, Tipperary, and Limerick, it would make a lively choice.

LENNON

Has already begun to be used as a baby name in tribute to Beatle John.

LONERGAN

The Lonergans have both an ecclesiastic and a musical heritage. It can also be spelled Lonagan or Lonegan.

LOWRY

Admirable family motto: "Virtue evergreen."

MacCORMAC

More unusual than its offshoot, Cormac.

MacCOY

A boy with this name would indeed be the real MacCoy (or McCoy).

MacDERMOT

Dating back to twelfth-century King Dermot of Moylurg, they were the only Irish family to have a princely title; a variation is now seen on screens via versatile actor Dylan McDermott.

MacSWEENEY

See Sweeney.

SOME MORE APPEALING MAC NAMES

• • •

MacAuley, MacBirney, MacCabe, MacClure, MacColum, MacDonagh, MacDonald, MacDonnell, MacGarry, MacGlynn, MacHugh, MacKeever, MacNeeley, MacNiell, MacQuade

MAGEE

Though it means "son of Hugh," Magee would have a broad and bouncy appeal for any Dad's son—or daughter.

MAGUIRE

This common surname has a lot of verve as a first, associated with several interesting figures, including Spider-Man Tobey.

MALONE

Classic surname with a lot of character.

MOLLOY

The title of a Samuel Beckett novel; this might also be spelled Malloy.

MOONEY

A name with two possible meanings: "dumb" or "wealthy." We'll opt for *wealthy*.

MOORE

Would make an elegant middle name.

MORRISSEY

Rocker (Steven Patrick) Morrissey made this a viable first name option.

MURPHY

It actually started life as a first name meaning "warrior of the sea," currently associated with charismatic blue-eyed actor Cillian.

NOLAN

This one's already entered the first-name column, most notably with baseball superstar Ryan (original first name: Lynn).

NUGENT

The term to "nugentize" dates back to poet Robert Nugent, who sustained himself by marrying wealthy widows to the point where he was able to lend money to King George III.

O'BRIEN

Based on the name of Brian Boru, the legendary tenth-century high king of Ireland and perfect for the grandson of a Brian.

O'CONNOR

Last name of countless eminent writers, entertainers, politicians, and diplomats.

O'GRADY

An American O'Grady was the great-grandfather of boxing immortal Muhammad Ali.

O'NEILL

Associated with the prominent American playwright Eugene O'Neill.

QUINN

Shades of "The Mighty Quinn"—a movie, a band, and a Bob Dylan song.

RAFFERTY

Already coolized by Jude Law and Sadie Frost as the name of their son.

REDMOND

Has a dash of danger, thanks to infamous highwayman Redmond O'Hanlon.

REAGAN/REGAN

President Ronald Reagan was one of many distinguished descendents of Brian Boru.

REILLY/RILEY

A huge unisex hit, used increasingly for girls.

RIORDAN (REER-dan)/REARDAN

Originated as a profession name for a royal poet.

ROONEY

Lighthearted name with meaningful meaning: "descendant of the hero."

SCULLY

You can pat yourself on the back with this name meaning "descendant of a scholar," which had a wide audience via the TV show *The X-Files*.

SHANAHAN

Has a lot more bounce and masculine dash than Shannon ever did.

SHERIDAN

Name of one of Ireland's wittiest playwrights, Richard Brinsley Sheridan.

SULLIVAN

Has a real twinkle in its eye; became a first name option when chosen for one of his twins by Patrick "McDreamy" Dempsey.

COOLEST
SURNAME
NAME
· · ·
Rooney

SWEENEY

An upbeat name that appears in the works of Yeats, T. S. Eliot, and Flann O'Brien—not to mention *Sweeney Todd*.

TIERNAN

The original Tiarnán was the name of early chieftains, kings, and princes.

TIERNEY

Like cousin Tiernan, a cool choice for either girls or boys.

breege

NICKNAME COOL

For the first time since the 1960s, nicknames have become a hot category of baby names, mostly those that are older, funkier diminutives with a Victorian pedigree. It's a trend that is quickly gathering momentum, with some of the names already having jumped onto the Irish popularity polls. Among those you can consider putting directly on the birth certificate:

girls

ABBIE/ABBY	CAIT
ADDIE	CASSIE
AGGIE	CLEO
BEA	COCO
BEESY	DAISY
BERNIE	DETTA
BIDDY	DIXIE
BREE	DOTTIE
BREEGE	EDIE
BRIDIE	EILY

ELLIE	RENNY
EVIE	ROSIE
FLORRIE	SADIE
GRACIE	SAM
IZZY	SIBBY
JAZ	SUKEY
JOSIE	TESSIE
KAT	TILLIE
KATIE	TRIONA (TREE-na)
KIT	
KITTY	boys
LETTY	
LIL	ALF
LOTTIE	ALFIE
LOU	ARCHIE
LULU	AUGIE
MAIDIE	BARNEY
MAISIE	BAZ
MAMIE	BEC
MO	BENNO
NELLY	BERNIE
NONIE	BILLY
PAITÍ (PAT-ee)	BRAN
PEIG (Peg)	BRY
PEIGÍ (PEG-ee)	CHARLIE
POLLY	CHRISTY
PRU	CON
	DEZ

DEZI	NED
DONN	NEILIE
EOCHO (YO-ko)	OLLIE
FLURRY	OZZIE
FREDDY	PADDY
GEORGIE	PAITI (PAT-ee)
GUS	RAY
JAMIE	SÉIMÍ (SHAY-mee)
JOHNNY	SHAY
KIT	SULLY
LACHIE (LOK-ee)	THAD
LOUIE	THEO
MAC	TULLY
MICK	WILL
MOSS	

fia

One of the coolest trends in the USA, now extending to other languages as well, is the rise of word names—words that, because they have a wonderful meaning and an appealing sound, make for fresh, evocative names. There's no reason this idea can't be translated into Irish as well. Here, some ideas for Irish words that might work as names. But this is just a beginning. Your imagination (and your dictionary) are the limit.

ABHAINN (Ah-WAN)	river
BRONNTANAS (BRUN-tan-is)	gift
CARRAIG (Korr-ig)	rock
CEART (Kee-art)	justice
EALA (A-la)	swan
ÉAN (Ee-an)	bird
EARRACH (A-ra)	spring
EILIT (EYE-lit)	doe
FEILEACÁN (Fel-li-CAWN)	butterfly
FEOTHAN (Fee-o-han)	breeze

FIA (FEE-ah)	deer
FÍRINNE (FEER-in-na)	truth
FOMHAIR (Foh-wir)	autumn
GEALACH (Gi-ahl-ukh)	moon
GEIMHREADH (GIV-roo)	winter
MUINÍN (Mwin-EEN)	trust
NÉAMH (NEYV)	heaven
RÉALTA (Ray-al-ta)	star
SAIBREAS (SEV-ris)	wealth
SAMHRADH (SAUR-a)	summer
SEODRA (Sho-dra)	jewel
SÍOCHÁIN (SHEE-a-kawn)	peace
SPÉIR (Spare)	sky
TONN	wave

grian

NAMES WITH COOL MEANINGS

Nature names, animal names, and names with uplifting or exciting meanings are cool in any language. A selection of Irish names with appealing meanings appears below:

girls

ÁINE (AH-nya)	radiance, splendor, brilliance
AISLING (ASH-ling)	dream, vision
AOIBHINN (EE-veen)	radiant beauty
AOIFE (EE-fa)	beautiful, radiant
BLÁTH (Blaw)	blossom
CAOIMHE (KEE-va)	comely, beautiful
CARMEL	garden
CAS/CASS/CASSIDY	curly haired
CATRIONA (Cat-REE-na)	pure
CROEB (KREV)	branch, garland
DANA/DANU (DA-noo)	abundance, wealth
DYMPHNA	a fawn

EIBHLÍN (EV-lin)	wished-for child
EINÍN (AY-neen)	little bird
FIAMAIN (FEE-vin)	swift-footed creature
FINNUALA (Fin-OO-la)	white shoulders
FÍONA/FINA	vine
FÍRINNE (FEER-een-ya)	truth
GEILÉIS (Gel-lis)/GELACE	bright swan
GRIAN (Gree-an)	sun
KEELY	graceful
LAOISE (LEE-sha)	radiant girl
LASAIR (LOH-sir)	flame
MAIRÉAD (Ma-REYD)	pearl
MUIRGHEAL (Mwir-ial)	bright as the sea
NIAMH (Neev)	radiance, brightness
NONÍN (No-NEEN)	daisy
ORLA	golden princess
OSNAIT (Os-nit)	little deer
REALTÁN (Rail-TAWN)	star
RÓISÍN (Ro-SHEEN)	little rose
SAOIRSE (SEER-sha)	freedom
SCOTH (Skoh)	bloom, blossom
SIBÉAL (Shib-ale)	wise woman
SÍLE (SHEE-la)	pure and musical
SÍOMHA (SHEE-ba)	peace
SIVE (rhymes with *five)*	sweetness, goodness
SLÁINE (SLOYNE-ye)/SLANY	health
SORCHA (SOR-ka or SOR-ra)	radiant

TEAGAN (TAY-gan)	beautiful
TUATHLA (TOO-la)	princess of the people

boys

AEDAL	highly courageous
ANBHILE (An-vile)	great tree
AODH (EY)	fire
AONGHUS (AING-gus)	true vigor, also an early Irish god of love
ART	bear
BRADEN	salmon
BROCK	badger
CADHAN (KEYE-an)	wild goose
CANA/CANNAGAN	wolf cub
CLOONEY	grassy meadow
COLM (KUL-um)/COLUM (KUL-um)	dove
CONÁN	great, high
CURRAN	hero, champion
DARRAGH (DA-ra)	like an oak
DECLAN (DEK-lan)	full of goodness
EILTÍN (Elt-een), ELTIN	young deer, lively person
FERGAL	valiant
LENNÁN	sweetheart, lover
LONÁN	blackbird
LONEGAN	bold, fierce
MARCÁN (Mar-kawn)	steed
MUGHRÓN (Moo-RONE)	lad of the seals

OISÍN (OH-sheen) /Ossian	little deer
OSCAR	deer lover
PEADAR (PAH-der)	rock
PHELIM (FEY-lim)	constant
QUINLAN	of beautiful shape
RONAN	little seal
SEAN	God's gracious gift
SORLEY	summer wanderer
TADGH (TYEg)	poet, philosopher

index

about the authors

Pamela Redmond Satran, who has been collaborating with Linda Rosenkrantz on baby name books for more than twenty years, is also the author of four novels: *Suburbanistas, Younger, Babes in Captivity,* and *The Man I Should Have Married.* She cowrites the popular "Glamour List" column for *Glamour* magazine and contributes frequently to such publications as *The New York Times, The Huffington Post,* and *The Daily Beast.* Pam lives with her husband and three children—daughter, Rory, and sons, Joe and Owen—near New York City. You can visit her Web site at www.pamelaredmondsatran.com.

Linda Rosenkrantz is the author of several non-name books, including *Telegram! Modern History as Told Through More Than 400 Witty, Poignant and Revealing Telegrams* and the memoir *My Life As a List: 207 Things About My (Bronx) Childhood;* and coauthor (with her husband, Christopher Finch) of *Gone Hollywood* and *Sotheby's Guide to Animation Art.* In addition to contributing articles to numerous magazines, she writes a nationally syndicated column on collectibles. She lives in Los Angeles and named her daughter Chloe.

Please visit their baby name Web site at www.nameberry.com.